MENTAL MEDICINE:

A Theoretical and Practical Treatise on Medical Psychology.

With an Essay on The New Age By William Al-Sharif

By

REV. W. F. EVANS

AUTHOR OF
Mental Cure

First published in 1872

This edition published by Read Books Ltd.
Copyright © 2019 Read Books Ltd.
This book is copyright and may not be
reproduced or copied in any way without
the express permission of the publisher in writing

British Library Cataloguing-in-Publication Data
A catalogue record for this book is available
from the British Library

"On earth there is nothing great but man;
In man there is nothing great but mind."

THE NEW AGE

An extract from the essay,
The New Age by William Al-Sharif

The 'industrial revolution', the 'Enlightenment Age' and colonialism had strengthened the power of the British Empire. Britain, in the second half of the nineteenth century, was probably the most powerful and influential empire in the world. The power of the empire, accompanied with the processes of modernisation and secularisation, created a new religious and cultural mental space. A 'New age' became part of cultural, religious and romantic imaginaire and represented a new era in which religion and culture would evolve in the favour of the empire and its British subjects. In 1843, The New Age was established in London. It proposed a society 'for the promotion of humanity and abstinence from animal food'. This society would also disseminate 'correct principles on universal peace, [and] health of soul and body'.

Christianity, in the age of the empire and missionary expansion, was influenced by the cultural aspirations for a 'new age'. Christian thinkers began to talk about a new age for 'the Lord' and Christianity. This 'new age' would fulfil biblical prophecies and embody new opportunities and truths for the Christian faith. Rationalist intellectuals imagined a new age for progress and science.

The philosophical and scientific criticism of Christianity, the elaboration of 'holistic' practices and theosophical ideas, the British colonialism of India and romantic Orientalism had all provided an inventive climate for the promotion of spiritualistic ideas. The process of modernisation and secularisation diminished the traditional authority of social and religious structures and shaped the transformation from the idea of destiny to choice and from providence to progress. Yet, there were individuals who opposed the religious hegemony of missionary societies and the hierarchal 'church religion' and sought spirituality in holism, occultism and esotericism. The individualised conquest of spirituality, which later influenced the New Age discourse, was formulated by modernism which invented 'the conception of a unique self and private identity, a unique personality and individuality, which can be expected to generate its own unique vision of the world'.

In the US, the 'New Age' imaginaire represented a new spiritual consciousness of the human self and was transformed by the ideas of Spiritualism, Transcendentalism, New Thought, Theosophy and Millenarianism. People such as Woodbury Melcher Fernald (1813-1873) and Warren Felt Evans (1817-1889) spoke of the coming of 'new age' spirituality. A weekly journal, New Age, was issued in San Francisco in 1865. The foundation of the Theosophical Society in 1875 in New York was significant for articulating theosophical concepts. This Society, which established its international headquarters in India, romanticised the religions of India and declared to challenge dogmatic religious authority and scientific materialism.

Despite the emergence of Christian evangelism and fundamentalism, the first three decades of the twentieth century witnessed numerous attempts by 'spiritual seekers' to create new spiritualities and seek new 'truths' for the 'new age'. Henry Jenkins says that the period between 1910 and 1935 was 'the first new age' and 'the period of emergence'.

PREFACE.

IN this volume the author has aimed to give the results of his study of Medical Psychology as a therapeutic agency, and the knowledge he has gained from many years' experience of the best methods of its application. He has not entered into a discussion of all the phenomena of the psychic force, but only those laws of its action that render it so efficient in the cure of all forms of mental and bodily disease. It contains the best light he could obtain, from every accessible source, in relation to this primitive and apostolic mode of healing the sick. The work is, in some degree, supplementary to the previous volume of the author on the mental aspect of disease and the psychological method of treatment. It contains information every one needs who has anything to do in the management and care of the sick, and which will qualify every person of ordinary intelligence to be his own family physician. It goes forth into the world with the hope that it may contribute some influence towards reviving this divine method of healing the sick, now wholly abandoned by the principal religious and sectarian organizations of the Christian world. May an age of living faith and spiritual power succeed the present reign of materialism and religious impotency, so that the so-called miracles of history may be reproduced as the common facts of our own age. It is to be hoped that the world will again witness the spectacle of the doings of men and women who are endued with power from on high, or whose natural faculties and abilities are reinforced and augmented by an influence emanating from the Central Life and the omnipresent spiritual realm of existence, intelligence and causation. Then miracles will cease to be such, from their frequency, and lose the element of wonder, when science reveals the laws by which they are effected. To "minister to a mind diseased," and thus to relieve and cure the multifarious forms of bodily disorder from the root, is the divinest work in which a human being was ever called to engage. May thousands of such followers of Jesus, the Christ, be raised up in a world of sickness and sorrow, pain and death, and qualified by the reception of his spirit to perform this sublime and sacred function, and thus stay, in some degree, the tide of misery that has overflowed our morally disordered globe.

As appropriate to the author's own feelings and to the subject he is about to discuss, he would adopt the language of the venerable Dr. Rush, as introductory to his work on the Diseases of the Mind: "In entering upon the subject of the following observations and inquiries, I feel as if I were about to tread upon consecrated ground. I am aware of its difficulty and importance, and I thus humbly implore that Being whose government extends to the thoughts of all his creatures, so to direct mine in this arduous undertaking, that nothing hurtful to my fellow-beings may fall from

PREFACE.

my pen, and that this work may be the means of lessening a portion of some of the greatest evils of human life."

No. 3 BEACON ST., BOSTON, MASS.
Oct. 12, 1872.

CONTENTS.

CHAPTER I.
The Gift and Art of Healing . . . . . . PAGE 11

CHAPTER II.
Qualifications of the Psychopathic Practitioner . . . 21

CHAPTER III.
Conditions of the Patient Favorable to a Cure . . . 31

CHAPTER IV.
The Conscious Impressible State 41

CHAPTER V.
How to Induce the Impressible State 47

CHAPTER VI.
Medical Psychology and the Limitations to its Abuse . . 55

CHAPTER VII.
PAGE
Auto-Magnetism or Self-Healing 68

CHAPTER VIII.
Phreno-Magnetism and its Use in Medical Psychology . . 73

CHAPTER IX.
Nervous Sensitiveness and Inharmonious Influences . . 80

CHAPTER X.
The Duality of the Mind and Body, and the Positive and Negative Distinction in the Psychic and Magnetic Forces of the Organism 88

CHAPTER XI.
The Brain, and Psychic and Nerve Centres 97

CHAPTER XII.
Effect of the Psychopathic Treatment of the Spine and Spinal Nerves 105

CHAPTER XIII.
The Application of the Psychic Force to the Epigastrium, and the Nature and Cure of Nervous Diseases . . 111

CHAPTER XIV.

The Abdominal Muscles, and the Mechanical Displacement of the Internal Organs 117

CHAPTER XV.

Nerve Conductors and their Use in Medical Psychology . 123

CHAPTER XVI.

The Agent in the Psychopathic Treatment and its Relation to the Vital Force 130

CHAPTER XVII.

Inanimate Objects and their Use in the Cure of Disease . 136

CHAPTER XVIII.

On the Law of Sympathy and its Application to the Cure of Mental and Bodily Disease 143

CHAPTER XIX.

How to Avoid Exhaustion and the Imbibing of the Diseased Condition of the Patient 151

CHAPTER XX.

Power from on High, or Spiritual Aid Necessary to Success in the Cure of Disease by Medical Psychology . . 160

CHAPTER XXI.

Miscellaneous Directions in the Treatment of Disease, including the Method of a Correct Diagnosis . . . 178

CHAPTER XXII.

Insanity and its Psychopathic Treatment 189

CHAPTER XXIII.

Remedies partly Mechanical and partly Psychopathic . . 201

CHAPTER XXIV.

Mental Medicine, or the Sanative Value of the Psychic Force 207

MENTAL MEDICINE.

CHAPTER I.

THE GIFT AND ART OF HEALING.

Reality of the Psychic Influence — Its Identity with the Vital Force — Why some have more Power to heal Disease than others — The Power not confined to a Few — Distinguished Healers — Greatrakes — George Fox — The Jewish Prophets — Jesus and the Apostles — In what Sense it is a Gift — How far an Art — Design of the Volume — Scientific Mission of the Present Age — Where the Psychopathic Method may be generally useful — Need of Popular Knowledge of its Nature and Laws — Change in the Condition of Human Nature — Modification of Diseases — New Remedial Agencies demanded — The Unseen.

IT is now an established fact, and has become a part of the positive science of the new age upon which humanity is entering, that one person can influence another person in a way usually called magnetic. The influence, thus imparted, is either identical with the vital force, or has the property of affecting its action. Some persons have more of this power than others, owing, perhaps, to their peculiar mental and physical organization, the ability to concentrate their mental energy and force upon a certain end or aim, and their superior strength of will. But the power to cure disease without the administration of medicines, and simply by the psychic force imparted through the hand, is a more common endowment than is generally supposed. A large proportion of both men and women, possessing an average share of intelligence, might become successful practitioners, with a little instruction, directing them how to use the powers they possess. In fact, a large number of persons of both sexes, in a quiet and unostentatious way, are successfully practising this apostolic mode of healing the sick without fee or reward, actuated solely by a benevolent desire of relieving human suffering, and by an irrepressible love of doing good. Some, by a more public career, have attracted general notice, and attained to fame. Such are scattered all along the world's history. Such were some of the Jewish prophets, who cured disease by this divine method. The remarkable cures wrought by Valentine Greatrakes, which attracted the attention of the English people, and which were investigated by the Royal Society, were effected by "stroking with the hands." George Fox, the founder of the Society of Friends or Quakers, performed, what have been deemed miracles of healing, as his Journal shows.

The cures wrought by Jesus were no miracles, or departures from the established order of nature, as he himself avers. They exhibit the action of a higher law, the dominion of mind over matter. Everything that is done is effected in harmony with some law of nature,— some law of mind or matter,— and has in it the relation of cause and effect. To understand the law by which it is done is to be able to do it. Hence, Jesus declares respecting his wonderful works, which were mostly those of healing the bodies and minds of the people who flocked to him from every part of the land of the Jews, "The works that I do shall ye do also, and greater works than these shall ye do, because I go to my

Father." This is as true as any promise that his lips ever uttered. He commissioned and instructed his apostles to "cure all manner of disease and sickness among the people." The same cause will produce the same effect to-day. The cures effected by Gassner, a Swiss clergyman, who created so wide-spread an excitement in the latter half of the 18th century, and those wrought by Madam Saint-Amour, a Swedenborgian lady of rank, in France, and those performed by Herr Richter, in Silesia, exhibit as great therapeutic power as was manifested by Jesus eighteen hundred years ago in Judea. All forms of disease were, in many cases, instantly healed by an invisible power or influence, and the wonders of the apostolic age were reproduced. Not that these persons possessed more power to cure disease than many others, but their natural gift was developed and cultivated by action, all their powers were consecrated to a divine use and to one work, and circumstances gave them notoriety. It is my opinion that hundreds and thousands of others possess equal power to heal disease, and, under like circumstances, would be equally successful.

The power of curing disease was conferred by the Christ upon the Church, not as a transient circumstance, attending the introduction of Christianity into the world, but as a perpetual inheritance. It was not so much a gift to individuals, as an invariable attribute of a vital faith. The Protestant clergy, in order to excuse and account to the world for their spiritual impotency, have strenuously argued that the gift was confined to the chosen twelve, or to the seventy disciples, or at most to the first century of the Christian Age. But without any limitation as to time or place, the risen Jesus affirms, "These signs shall follow *them that believe*. In my name they shall cast out demons; they shall speak with new tongues; they shall take up serpents, and if they shall drink any deadly thing, it shall not hurt them; they shall lay hands on the sick, and they shall recover." (Mark 16: 17, 18.) This wondrous power is here by a divine commission conferred upon all men in every age and clime, who truly believe, who have a faith whose vital root is the life of God in the soul of man. As William Howitt has well said, "If these things are not true, Christianity is not true; if it and they are true, the fault lies in ourselves if we lack the power; we have not vital faith, and are only half Christians." Nine-tenths of the public life of Christ was spent in curing diseases of mind and body. To truly follow Christ is to do the same thing, moved to it by the same spirit of love and all-conquering faith. He who does this is in the genuine apostolic succession, though no lordly prelate has ever laid his impotent hands upon his head. He who cannot do it is only half a Christian minister, and that the smallest half, though he may have been ordained by the pope, or even St. Peter himself. Such men are vainly striving, after the example of Gehazi, the servant of Elijah, to raise a dead world to life, by laying upon it the staff of the prophet, rather than by the indwelling power of the God of all the prophets.

The possession of this power is at the same time a divine gift and an art. It is a gift of God, so far as any one has a natural adaptation to this Christlike work, arising from constitutional peculiarities of mental and physical organization. Among the *charismata*, or spiritual gifts, enumerated by Paul, is found the gift of healing, which is not something superadded to a man's natural possessions, but is only the development of a power arising from a peculiarity of mental structure, by which an individual is naturally fitted for the work of healing.

It is also an art, for knowledge is power. To know how to do a thing is to be able to do it. He who best understands the laws of the psychic force in its application to the cure of disease, by availing himself of that knowledge, and thus adapting his treatment to nature's immutable laws, will greatly add to his efficiency in the cure of all morbid conditions. The author has received numerous letters from all parts of the country, asking for instruction in the use of the gift of healing, which many persons have an inward consciousness of possessing. To give the necessary information in the brief limits of an epistolary correspondence was found impracticable. It is the design of the present work to give, in a condensed form, a clear statement of the laws of Medical Psychology, so far as they relate to the cure of disease, and to give a few simple directions in the use of this wonderful healing power. There are multitudes of men and women who have the "gift of healing," and the possession of a particular gift is a divine call to use it. They lack only the knowledge which is necessary to an efficient use of the power with which they are endowed. We write for the benefit of this numerous class of persons, who, in a humble way, and unknown to fame, are striving to follow Jesus, and do the works he did, and who recognize as one of the signs of a genuine faith, that "they shall lay hands upon the sick and they shall recover." It is a part of the scientific mission of the present age to disrobe the so-called miracles of past centuries of all their mystery, and reduce them to the operation of known laws, and thus render them credible as historical facts, and their repetition practicable at the present time. The science of human magnetism, which is adequate to this result, is not a mere plaything, designed to amuse and astonish a popular audience, but is one of the best gifts of God to man. Its intelligent employment as a curative agency will be fruitful in blessings to the world, in alleviating suffering, and curing diseases of mind and body.

There are many cases of disease, for which a physician is employed, that might be almost instantly relieved, especially in their incipient stage, by a judicious psychopathic treatment administered by some member of the family, if they only had the needed instruction in the use of this efficient therapeutical agency, which it is the design of this work to afford. I do not affirm, or believe, that this system of medical psychology will cure every form of disease, but I do assert what I know to be true, that dealing as it does with the vital force itself, it operates more immediately and efficiently in relieving pain, and restoring the lost harmony in the action and distribution of the organic forces, in which all disease consists, than any remedy known to medical science. And where it will not cure, it always benefits and never injures the patient.

The world is undergoing a change. We live in one of those mighty transitionary epochs of human history, when old things are passing away and all things are becoming new. We are realizing the fulfilment of the prophetic announcement of ages ago, that God would pour out his spirit upon all flesh. This divine afflatus is coming out of the opening and descending heavens upon the whole human family, quickening into life dormant faculties, and opening the organism to all invisible, imponderable and spiritual influences and forces. In the dreary ages of the past, men have been like the sturdy oak, that defied the strength of the hurricane's blast, it was so firmly anchored in the coarse, hard soil of the earth, but now, like the mimosa, they shrink from the slightest touch of the finger of spirit-power. God and the angel world are rolling away the rock of a base sensuality and carnality from the sepulchre of the sleeping spirit, and, obedient to the voice of Omnipotent Love, it is coming forth with spontaneous alacrity in the renewed powers of a risen humanity. Men everywhere are becoming increasingly susceptible to magnetic and psychological impression. The selfish isolation of men from each other is coming to an end. Individuals, communities, and nations invisibly affect each other, and are becoming more and more bound in the same bundle of life. What we see in the outward world, in the increased facilities of intercommunication between distant individuals and peoples by means of steam-navigation and the electro-magnetic telegraph, is only the ultimation in the realm of sense of an antecedent closer relation and connection effected in the world of mind or spirit. This increased susceptibility and impressibility to magnetic and psychic influences, which mankind now everywhere exhibit, which renders them so delicately sensitive to every breath of the spirit that blows upon them from above or beneath, must necessarily be attended with more or less disorder, mental and physical, but is certainly educating humanity to a higher range of life and activity. It is giving rise to a new class of diseases, that baffle the skill of the old practitioners, and the medical science of past ages can only look upon the patient in dumb amazement and silent impotency. It is a fact, patent to every one who will open his eyes to observe, that disease is now, far more than formerly, mental and nervous in its origin and characteristics. The old works on Therapeutics and Materia Medica are now of little more use in this altered condition of human nature than is a last year's almanac in navigation. This increased sensitiveness to psychic and spiritual influences, which characterizes and underlies the diseases of the present age, must be met by more subtle remedies, on a different application of the principle of Hahnemann, that like cures like. A new school of medicine is slowly growing up to meet this want. The Psychopathic physician, discarding all drugs and chemical agencies, communicates the subtle magnetic and spiritual forces, to nerve up and tone up the organism with a higher vitality, quickening dormant functions and reconstructing impaired ones. He inoculates the patient with a sanative contagion, and impregnates the system with a new and improved vital force, that gives birth to health and harmony. The use of these spiritual dynamic forces, even in the hands of the ignorant and imperfectly educated practitioner, is attended with a success that many a learned physician has sought in vain, and sometimes performs cures, in the presence of which the so-called, diplomatized medical science of the day stands in dumb amazement. These will be more frequent in the progress and spread of a higher knowledge of the once mysterious vital principle, and the imponderable forces that impel the organic machinery. While all diseases, through the emanative sphere that surrounds a patient, are to a certain extent contagious, through the law of sympathy, so life, health, and happiness are equally communicative. Our connection with the universal and ever-present spiritual world is a vital one, as Swedenborg taught more than a century ago; and as the unbarred heavens come into closer proximity with earthly conditions they will bring down to mankind a higher and happier physical and mental existence, to constitute the basis of the advanced spiritual life which is being gradually unfolded, as the influence of the light and heat of day and the gentle dews of night unroll the bud into the full-blown flower. Jesus directed and empowered his disciples, as they entered into any city, "to heal the sick that were therein, and say unto them, The kingdom of God is come nigh unto you."

THE UNSEEN.

"About us float the odorous gales
   That kiss the eternal hills of day:
Oh that the chilling fog would lift
   And show our waiting feet the way!

"We grope about us — seeing not
   The waiting ones outside our sight,
Whose viewless hands are clasping ours,
   To lead us up the shining height!

"We may not know the cords we touch,
   That, glancing 'long the electric line,
Flash back upon our sodden lives
   Some hints of peace and love divine.

"As clefted mountains sometimes hide
   Behind the vapor's purpling drift,
Till, pierced by Sol's directer ray,
   Their girdling shadows slowly lift:

"So we grope on, 'neath fogs of doubt,
   Our hearts in solemn silence bowed;
While God's eternal verities
   Are hidden from us by a cloud

"When, lo! a kindling glory throws
   A sudden splendor o'er our way,
And, slowly lifting, lo, appear
   The whitely shining hills of day!

"And yet not oft — nor yet to all,
 These prophecies and hints are given;
Only as signals, sparsely set,
 Along the battlements of heaven.

"Yet some day, every waiting soul
 Shall see the mists slow rolling back,
And, freed from clogs of earth and sin,
 Walk calmly up the shining track!"

CHAPTER II.

QUALIFICATIONS OF THE PSYCHOPATHIC PRACTITIONER.

Importance of his Mental States — The Higher Faculties — Usefulness of Medical Science — Great Physical Strength not Necessary — A Child will cure a Man — The Necessity of Faith — Whence derived — Sanative Virtue of Love — The Model Healer — Power from above — The Light of Life.

THE person who would successfully use the psychopathic method in the cure of disease should be one of high mental and moral character, and actuated solely or mainly by the love of doing good, that he may be worthy of the trust reposed in him, and that the interests committed to his charge may be safe in his hands. A person's psychic influence will partake of his predominant phrenological organs, and will be tinged with the quality of his ruling loves. He infects his patients with his own habitual mental states. He impregnates the subject with the sphere of his own life, — his modes of thought and feeling. It is the higher faculties that possess the power of imparting a sanative virtue and influence. The nearer one approaches the character of Jesus, and the more he is in sympathetic union with him, the more power he will possess to " heal all manner of sickness and disease among the people." He was everybody's best friend. The prevailing mental states of the practitioner are of far more importance than his physical force, or even the state of his health. The cure of disease by this method is effected more by a psychological or spiritual force, than by any material influence. Hence this mode of treating disease I call Psychopathy, or the mental-cure. It is the triumph of mind over matter, of the spiritual over the material. And the patient's own mind has much more to do with it than many suppose.

He ought also to have an adequate knowledge of the anatomy and physiology of man, especially of the nervous system. He should understand the nature and symptoms of disease, the relation of the mind to the body, and the influence of the one upon the other. He should be especially skilled in the knowledge of the causes of disease, for every morbid condition of the body is an effect, of which something is the cause. This anterior cause must be removed before the effect will cease. There is no system of medical practice, that requires a profounder knowledge of human nature, both in its physical and spiritual departments, than the psychological method of healing. But all do not possess this, and much can be done without it. Many physicians of all schools enter upon an extensive practice of the healing art, with only a small capital of brains.

It has been demonstrated by experiment that in order to the production of the highest psychopathic and curative effect, great physical strength is not necessary in the physician. Madam Hauffé, the Seeress of Prevorst, had a wonderful therapeutic influence, though herself a confirmed and hopeless invalid. It is rather the difference in the magnetic condition of the operator and subject. In producing the magnetic sleep, a child will sometimes do it, when the subject is a strong man, sooner than another man of equal physical force could do it. The greater the difference in the psychic or magnetic condition, the more marked will be the effect.

How often has a child cured a headache in a man, by passing his hands caressingly over his brain and through his hair! The highest and most immediate results are witnessed where the one is as positive as the other is negative.

He who would cure diseases of mind and body, by psychic and spiritual force, must have faith in God. When the disciples of Jesus found themselves unable to cure a certain case of insanity and obsession, on inquiring the cause of their inefficiency, he replied, " Because of your *unbelief.*" (Matt. 17: 20.) In another place he directed them, as a qualification for executing their commission, to heal all manner of sickness and disease among the people, to have faith in God, or, as it is rendered in the margin, with literal exactness, " Have the faith of God," — a faith divinely imparted. Such a faith is not only one of the essential conditions of a strong volition, but connects the soul with the Central Life, and augments the power of every faculty of the human mind. It puts the soul in vital conjunction with the divine omnipotence. The Christian world has never fully understood the power of a living faith. Jesus does not exaggerate or overstate its force, when he affirms, " If thou canst believe, all things are possible to him that believeth." (Mark 9: 23.) It reinforces human weakness with the divine creative power. Without it, whatever qualifications we may possess, " there shall be no might in thine hand." (Deut. 28: 32.) It invests the soul with a serene consciousness of power, and there can be no substitute for the eternal calmness that closes round the mind of him who dwells in God.

The psychopathic practitioner must have confidence in his own ability. He must be a man of Abrahamic *faith.* He can do nothing without it. To doubt is to fail. A want of faith is weakness. This confidence ought not to be an inordinate self-esteem, which is repugnant to every healthy moral nature, but may arise from a calm consciousness of a knowledge of the laws of human nature, and of the power with which such knowledge invests the mind of man. It may spring from a deep conviction of the purity of our motives, and the aid of invisible powers. It must also have its root in love, — a love so great, so divine, as to be willing to lay down life itself, that others might live, and to bear the burdens and share the pains of others. Here is the secret of the success of Jesus. His maxim was, "The good shepherd giveth his life for the sheep." Love is the inmost vital principle of man. It is life itself. He who has the highest and divinest degree of it will be the most successful in healing the sick by the application of the principles of medical psychology. It is a spark of the divine life itself. A bad man may administer drugs, but an individual radically false, selfish, and morally rotten, cannot cure disease by this divine method. The loss of psychological power, arising from a course of moral and intellectual disorder, is one of the divinely appointed safeguards of this important agent against its being perverted to purposes of evil. The sublime calmness of an evenly balanced mind, the possession of a self-respect resulting from intellectual and moral elevation, perfect self-control, and presence of mind, the power of concentrating the mental and will-force, a stubborn faith that is ready to grapple with seeming impossibilities, a facility in adapting one's self to the condition and wants of all persons, a profound knowledge of human nature, an ardent love of doing good, and a spirit of kindness that condescends to the poor and longs to lift up its hands and call down a blessing upon every human being, are the essential elements in the character of the successful psychopathic practitioner.

To attain the highest success in the treatment of diseases of mind and body, we must be in sympathetic conjunction with Christ and the realm of life above, and be endued with power from on high. The spirit world, the home of the blessed, and the seat of all causation, is not far off in some starry world, in a distance so remote that no telescope can empower the natural eye to pierce its dimness. The truly spiritual man is in close proximity and affinity with the society of the angel bands. He has sought and found the ever-present kingdom of the heavens. He dwells on the border-land between the two worlds, where they so touch and unite, that where earth ends and heaven begins cannot be clearly defined. Death to such is an empty name, a sound without a meaning. They live eternal life. They live and move in the antechamber of the celestial habitation. And so may we.

> " I cannot hide that some have striven,
> Achieving calm, to whom was given
> The joy that mixes man with heaven
>
> " Who, rowing hard against the stream,
> Saw golden gates of Eden gleam,
> And did not dream it was a dream.
>
> " But looking upward, full of grace,
> They prayed, and from a happy place,
> God's glory smote them on the face;
>
> " Then heard, by secret transport led,
> Even in the charnels of the dead,
> The murmur of the fountain-head.

"They seemed to hear a heavenly Friend,
And through thick veils to apprehend
A labor working to an end.

"Heaven opens inward, chasms yawn,
Vast images in glimmering dawn,
Half shown, are broken and withdrawn."

He who would impart a sanative spiritual virtue to others, minister to a mind diseased, pluck from the heart a rooted sorrow, and perform the highest, holiest, and divinest function of human nature, in relieving diseases of mind and body, and by his voluntary activity and silent influence communicate health, harmony, and happiness, must himself be in sympathy with the fountain of life and light, not as an occasional transport, by which a soul is carried out of its natural element, but as an habitual and confirmed state. As Thomas à Kempis remarks, " He who would impart peace to others, must have peacefulness himself." He must breathe the atmosphere of the divine and heavenly, and dwell in the suburbs of the celestial city. He must attain to an interior state where the inner ear can catch the echo of thought and life in the morning-land. He must receive thence that he may impart, and ask only that he may have wherewith to give. I do not mean that we should come to open communion with *individual* spirits, which may not be desirable until we are unfolded to that degree of the inner life that shall render it natural and safe, when the latent powers of the interior manhood can no longer be confined in its chrysalis condition, and asserts its freedom, but I mean a fellowship and conscious communication with the general sphere of life and intelligence in the ever-present heavens. We must be admissive of the *light of life*. In speaking of this universal sphere of light and love, under the expressive designation of the Logos or Word, as it is the secret animating principle of all language, it is said, "In it is life, and the life is the light of men." This living light of the heavens, received by us, ultimates itself in thought and emotion, and these in words, so far as our external language is able to embody and express them. In the other world, language is only the communication of the living thoughts of one mind to another. In certain states of mental abstraction, we may come into a condition where the ideas of the higher range of existence and intelligence may consciously flow into us, as the flower imbibes the light and heat of the morning sun. Some persons, in whom the religious and spiritual nature has been highly unfolded, and the inner manhood has attained to freedom from material restraint and limitation, have thus received life and light from the upper world, the soul imbibing the thoughts and feelings of the angelic realms. Such was that most remarkable man, Emanuel Swedenborg. And how large a share of our best thoughts and most hallowed desires and emotions come to us from this source, we know not, but doubtless far more than a sensuous world is prepared to believe or admit. On the language of the world of spirit, in harmony with which we receive light from above, Frederic Von Schlegel, in his profound treatise on the Philosophy of Life and Philosophy of Language, thus remarks: "If, as we cannot but suppose, a communication does take place among those spiritual beings, who in intelligence are preferred to man, then must the immediate speech of these spirits be very different from our half-sensuous, half-rational, half-earthly, half-heavenly language of nature and humanity. For even as spiritual, it cannot but be immediate, — never employing figure and those grammatical forms which human language first analyzes to form again out of them new and fresh compounds. According to the two properties which constitute the essence of mind (*geist*), it can only be a communication, a transmission, an awakening or immission of thought — some wholly definite thought — by the will, or else the communicating, exciting, and producing by the thought of some equally definite volition. It may be that something of this, or at least something not absolutely dissimilar, occurs in human operations. It is possible that this immediate language of mind, as a secret and invisible principle of life, — as a rare and superior element, — is contained also in human language, and, as it were, veiled in the outer body, which, however, becomes visible only in the effects of a luminous and lofty eloquence, in which is displayed the magic force of language and of a ruling and commanding thought."

Swedenborg in his numerous works, in which he unfolds the laws that govern all spirit life, often refers to this immediate language of mind, the *cogitatio loquens*, or thought-speaking. But we are ourselves spirits in all that is essential to our existence, and with our inner nature adjusted in harmony with all that is divine and heavenly, may receive the inflowing of life and light from God and the angel-world. And with the soul blissfully fixed on its divine centre, we may peacefully revolve around it in an ever-widening orbit of activity and usefulness. What the religious world most needs to-day is not the knowledge of the historic Jesus, and a faultless creed, but a vital union with the risen and ascended Christ, who has gone up on high and received gifts for men; and most of all we need to receive from him the quickening influence of the baptism of the holy spirit and of fire. This makes the recipient of it "a burning and shining light," and a divine power among men.

"Onward he moves, disease and death retire,
And murmuring demons hate him, but admire."

Without this, the Church, with all its solemn pomp of externality, is like painted fire, which looks well, but emits no living light and heat. Its creed, however orthodox, is like moonbeams reflected from polar ice; and all its organized activities are but the spasmodic movements of a galvanized corpse; and all its members, however wealthy and respectable, are to the truly spiritual eye like the dry and bleaching bones of the valley in the vision of the prophet. The baptism of the spirit, or the reception of the sphere of life and light from God and the angel-world, augments and stimulates all the dormant powers of our inner nature, and heightens the vital activity of every department of our complex being. It quickens the intellect by warming the heart, clears the mental vision from thickest films of sensuality and carnality, and on the sightless spiritual orbs, veiled in the natural man and oppressed with night, it pours celestial day. It endues the subject of it "with power from on high," and in the sphere of benevolent and Christian activity makes him an embodiment and instrument of a fraction of God's omnipotent love; and in a world of sickness and sorrow, pain and death, where the spiritual atmosphere is tremulous with the heart-throbbings of despair, and every breeze is laden and heavy with the echoes of sighing grief, he moves on in his beneficent career, unostentatiously accomplishing the divinest result, like the noiseless but potent forces of nature.

His outward life is but the manifestation in act and deed of "the stirrings of deep divinity within." In a mitigated sense, he can say: "The spirit of the Lord God is upon me; because the Lord hath anointed me to preach good tidings unto the meek; he hath sent me to bind up the broken-hearted, to proclaim liberty to the captives, and the opening of the prison to them that are bound; to proclaim the acceptable year of the Lord; to comfort all that mourn; to give them beauty for ashes, the oil of joy for mourning, and the garment of praise for the spirit of heaviness." (Isa. 61: 1–3.)

CHAPTER III.

CONDITIONS OF THE PATIENT FAVORABLE TO A CURE.

Faith in the Remedial Agency — How far Necessary — Knowledge better than Faith — Desire to get Well — Consent of Will — No Repugnance to Psychopathy — Passivity Necessary — How Medical Psychology sometimes Operates to Cure Disease — There should be no Fear of It — Mental Influence in Disease — Testimony of Dr. Forbes Winslow — M. Reveillé-Parise — Schiller — Dr. Sweetser — Feuchtersleben.

THERE are certain conditions of the patient, which, if not absolutely necessary to a cure, are extremely favorable to such a result. Among these mental states may be mentioned some degree of faith in the efficiency of the psychopathic method, and the ability of the practitioner to afford relief and effect a cure. The stronger this faith is, the greater the probability of success. The effect of faith and hope are always salutary. But so far as my own observation and experience go, in the treatment of the sick, these mental conditions are no more necessary to a cure than they are in any system of medication. Faith in the remedial agent, whatever it may be, always increases its efficiency. But the psychopathic physician has the advantage of all other practitioners in his ability to control the mental states of his patients. This is of more importance than all the drugs that ever were administered. This is coming to be the *secret* opinion of the most intelligent physicians of the day. Where faith and hope do not exist in the patient, it must be the first business of the physician to induce those mental conditions. How it may be done, we shall show hereafter.

An intelligent appreciation of the laws of what is called magnetism, from the want of a proper name, is far better than a blind faith. Knowledge is the highest form of faith. It is the perfection of faith, as where I believe two and two are four. It is always desirable to make the patient understand the reason for everything you do for him. The whole subject should be divested of all mystery. It should be understood, at the outset, that you propose to work no miracle by magical and mysterious agencies, but to effect a cure in harmony with nature's laws. The subject should be explained and brought within the comprehension of the invalid. It may take time to do this; but it is time well spent. The most salutary faith a patient can possess is a boundless confidence in the laws of nature, in accordance with which the divine power acts, and you propose to afford him help.

We may further remark, that it is essential that the patient have a desire to get well. This desire may be inordinate and amount to a morbid anxiety and impatience, which is an unfavorable state. There may be, and often is, a restless haste to be cured. Such persons cannot wait, they must be cured in the twinkling of an eye. The first step toward a cure, by any system of medicine, would be to remove this diseased mental state, and prescribe those excellent remedies in chronic disease, time and patience. But a desire to get well, if it be not inordinate, is essential to a cure. It is one of the laws of our being, that desire for a thing renders us receptive of it.

There ought not only to be a desire of recovery, but a willingness to get well in this way. There should be no repugnance to Medical Psychology as a curative agency. If a person is not sick enough to be *willing* to get well by a course of psychopathic treatment, the remedy will act with greatly diminished efficiency. There are certain persons, who, for some unaccountable reason, have a deep-seated antipathy, and an intense horror of the psychopathic treatment, and all its phenomena. To see a person in the somnambulic state makes them unhappy, and they have a repugnance to it. They can give no reason for it, nor raise any solid objection to it. Such persons often remark that they had rather die than get well by the use of so intangible a remedy. They ought to have their choice. They had better take drugs, if they prefer them, — the more nauseous the better. Let them be vomited, purged, depleted, salivated, or subjected to any other effect of allopathic medication.

There must be a mutual understanding and confidence between the physician and the patient. The latter must deliver himself up *passively* to the former, who ought to be worthy of the confidence reposed in him. A state of *passivity* is of far more importance than faith, or any peculiarity of temperament. I have never been able to see that much importance was to be attached to the temperament of the subject. It may be true that some temperaments are more easily influenced by the psychic force than others; but I have never yet found a person of any temperament, who could not be affected more or less, both mentally and physically, by it, provided he passively and without reserve surrendered himself to the action of this invisible and potent agent.

The patient ought also to be sufficiently enlightened

with regard to the nature and effects of Medical Pychology as not to be alarmed at any symptoms that may arise. *Sometimes*, though quite rarely, the most favorable effects may be produced, when a person *feels* worse after the psychopathic treatment. It increases the effort of nature to overcome the morbid state, assists the reaction of the vital force against the unnatural condition of things in the system, and consequently occasions an increased disturbance in the bodily functions, hurries on the natural crisis of the disease, and brings the spiritual evils and abnormal mental states, underlying the disordered physiological action of the organic structure, to a culmination. The result of all this is, the patient feels worse when he is actually better. His sensations are no sure guide to a correct judgment and diagnosis of his real condition. This effect is, as before remarked, quite rare, and should cause no alarm in either the physician or patient. The usual effect of an application of Medical Psychology is an immediate relief of all painful sensations and uncomfortable symptoms. If one has taken into the stomach some sickening and poisonous drug, under the direction of the family physician, even if he is drugged to the very verge of death itself, he is not frightened at the result. He patiently endures the effects, because they are what he expected. If this sanative spiritual agent *occasionally* hurries on the natural crisis of the disease, and the patient temporarily feels worse, let no one be alarmed. Under the direction of unerring nature, it will come to a desirable consummation. Where the proper mental conditions exist in the patient, the psychopathic method of cure, under the direction of an intelligent and judicious physician, will be found one of the most efficient remedies for nearly every form of chronic disease within the whole realm of nature.

In all painful conditions of the system the patient must be instructed and empowered to divert his thoughts from himself and his state. It is a physiological axiom that there is no sensation, at least no perception of sensation, without attention or directed consciousness to the part. It is a prescription that comes to all the diseased and unhappy from the wisdom of the upper realm of mind, that we can never get well until we stop *thinking* we are sick. To break up the confirmed habit of thinking that we are diseased, and to cease dwelling, in thought or word, upon our unhappy state, will remove the spiritual cause of our disease, and the bodily malady will disappear like darkness before the rising sun.

The patient must learn the importance of checking the morbid inclination to *speak* of his troubles and his diseased condition. It is a law of our nature that to express a feeling in words intensifies it. There is often witnessed in nervous invalids a selfish tendency to dwell upon their sufferings, to expatiate with mournful eloquence upon their pains, and to exaggerate the miseries of their situation. This must be checked. As Dr. Reid has truly remarked, "By endeavoring, from benevolent motives, to smother the expression of our sorrows, we often mitigate their inward force. If we cannot imbibe the spirit, it is often profitable, as well as good-natured hypocrisy, to put on the appearance of cheerfulness.

" 'By *seeming* gay, we grow to what we seem.' "

The mental state of the patient is not a matter of secondary importance. The morbid state of mind, in most chronic invalids, is the underlying cause of their pathological condition, and demands the first attention of the physician. This is frankly acknowledged by many distinguished practitioners of medicine, but at the same time they make no practical use of the truth. Dr. Forbes Winslow remarks: "The physician is daily called upon, in the exercise of his profession, to witness the powerful effects of mental emotion upon the material fabric. He recognizes the fact, although he may be unable to explain its rationale. He perceives that mental causes induce disease, destroy life, retard recovery, and often interfere with the successful operation of the most potent remedial means exhibited for the alleviation and cure of bodily disease and suffering. Although such influences are admitted to play an important part, either for good or for evil, I do not conceive that, as physicians, we have sufficient appreciation of their great importance." (*Journal of Psychological Medicine*, Vol. vii., p. 107.)

In his work on Moral Therapeutics, M. Reveillé-Parise more fully admits the influence of the mind on the body in the generation of disease. "If a patient dies, we open his body, rummage among the viscera, and scrutinize most narrowly all the organs and tissues, in the hope of discovering lesions of some sort or another; there is not a small vessel, membrane, cavity, or follicle, which is not attentively examined, — the color, the weight, the thickness, the volume, the alteration, — nothing escapes the eye of the studious anatomist. He handles, touches, smells, and looks at everything; then he draws his conclusions one way or another. One thing only escapes his attention; that is, he is looking at merely organic effects, forgetting all the while that he must mount higher up to discover their causes. These organic alterations are observed, perhaps, in the body of a person who has suffered deeply from mental distress and anxiety; these have been the energetic cause of his decay, but they cannot be discovered in the laboratory or amphitheatre. Many physicians of extensive experience are destitute of the ability of searching out the mental causes of disease; they cannot read the book of the heart, and yet it is in this book that are inscribed, day by day, and hour by hour, all the griefs, and all the miseries, and all the vanities, and all the fears, and all the joys, and all the hopes of man, and in which will be found the most active and incessant principle of that frightful series of organic changes which constitute pathology. This is quite true, — whenever the equilibrium of our mental nature is long or very seriously disturbed, we may rest assured that our animal functions will suffer. Many a disease is the *contre-coup*, so to speak, of a strong moral emotion; the mischief may not be apparent at the time, but its germ will be nevertheless inevitably laid."

All this is most certainly true, and commends itself with self-evidencing force to the consciousness of every invalid, especially those of a nervous type of disease. I know of no work in the whole range of medical science which gives due prominence to the influence of the mind over the nervous system in causing disease. The treatise of Whytt on the nervous system makes the nearest approach to it, but falls short of the mark. Yet it is a truth of great practical value, that will in the future be fully recognized, and its recognition must essentially modify the practice of medicine. We can say in the language of Schiller, "A physician whose horizon is bounded by an historical knowledge of the human machine, and who can distinguish terminologically and locally the coarser wheels of this intellectual clock-work, may be, perhaps, idolized by the mob; but he will never raise the Hippocratic art above the narrow sphere of a mere bread-earning craft."

It is remarked by Dr. William Sweetser, in his excellent work on Mental Hygiene, that " the influence of the intellect and the passions upon the health and endurance of the human organization has been but imperfectly understood and appreciated in its character and importance by mankind at large. Few, we believe, have formed any adequate estimate of the sum of bodily ills which have their source in the mind. Those of the medical profession even, concentrating their attention upon the physical, are too prone to neglect the mental causes of disease; and thus may patients be subjected to the harshest medicines of the pharmacopœia, the true origin of whose malady is some inward sorrow, which a moral balm alone can reach."

The spiritual nature of man is the governing, controlling principle in his outward organism, and in its varying states is the cause of the body's health or malady. Feuchtersleben, in his profound work on the Principles of Medical Psychology, in speaking of the influence of the mind on the body, says: " Even the material nature of man is not wholly material; his very organization is calculated for his higher destination; and it may be affirmed, that not only the philosopher, but the naturalist, if he would duly understand the physical nature of man, must be strongly impressed with this truth. Body and mind are most intimately blended in every part of the structure of the living individual; and as the disorders of the mind are often removed by pharmaceutical remedies, so, on the other hand, the diseases of the body as frequently require the aid of the psychological physician. In disorders of the nerves especially, the physician can often effect nothing, if he do not in the first place direct his treatment to the mind. The numerous varying symptoms which, under the name of spasms, act so conspicuous a part in pathology, and unhappily a still more conspicuous part in real life, are often removed most successfully and effectually by judiciously directing, controlling, and taking advantage of the state of the mind; and how few disorders there are of any organic system in which the nerves do not at least symptomatically suffer. We see, therefore, how extensive is the application of psychical methods of cure throughout the whole domain of the healing art." (*Medical Psychology*, p. 9.)

The mind is never agitated by any strong affection or emotion, without a sensible change immediately ensuing in some one or more of the vital phenomena, and which, according to its nature, or the circumstances under which it occurs, may be either morbid or sanative in its effects. All inharmonious psychological influences in the social relations and surroundings of an invalid, and the disorderly influences of the ever-present world of spirits, intensify his sufferings and retard the process of his recovery. I have had many patients laboring under the most serious nervous disturbance, amounting to an almost positive insanity, arising solely from their extreme susceptibility to the unseen influence of a low order of spiritual intelligences. It is a fruitful source of mental and nervous disorders. I am confirmed in the truth of the opinion of Swedenborg, whose open intercourse with the spirit-world for a period of more than a quarter of a century, qualified him to judge, that communion with individual spirits is attended with peril to both body and soul, unless we are first protected by union with Jesus, the Christ. To save men from all disorderly mental and spiritual influence constituted his divine mission to the world, and a work he still delights to perform, and to empower his disciples to do. A conscious and permanent union with him is at the same time our highest attainable spiritual state, and our protection from the presence and influx of spirits that would otherwise cause a loss of mental equilibrium, and a corresponding disturbance of the bodily functions. In the enjoyment of the calm happiness of unbroken fellowship with him, and vitally united to him as the branch to the vine, and sheltered by his all-surrounding presence and love, "the gates of hell shall not prevail against us."

THE MANIFESTATION OF JESUS.

"His robe was white as flakes of snow
  When through the air descending;
I saw the clouds beneath him melt,
  And rainbows o'er him bending!
And then a voice — no, not a voice —
  A deep and calm revealing
Came through me, like a vesper strain
  O'er tranquil waters stealing.

"And ever since that countenance
  Is on my pathway shining,
A sun from out a higher sky,
  Whose light knows no declining;
All day it falls upon my road,
  To keep my feet from straying,
And when at night I lay me down,
  I fall asleep while praying."

CHAPTER IV.

THE CONSCIOUS IMPRESSIBLE STATE.

Mistake of the Early Practitioners — Difficulty of inducing the Sleep — A Subject may be fully Magnetized without it — Constitutional Sensitiveness — The Test of it — The Impressible State described — Physiological Influence of Mental Force — The Power of Suggestion — Therapeutic Value of the Impressible State — Permanency of the Effects.

THE early practitioners, from Mesmer downward, labored under an error in supposing that the somnambulic sleep was necessary to the efficiency of magnetism as a curative agency. In this way much time was wasted and labor lost, as many patients cannot be put into the sleep without long and repeated efforts, and on some the sleep cannot be induced at all. It often requires as many as twenty sittings, and even more, before some patients will exhibit the phenomena of the complete somnambulic state. Those who are the most successful in the cure of disease seldom or never aim to produce the state of coma or insensibility. In fact, it is now well established that a subject may be perfectly magnetized, and will exhibit all the prominent phenomena of the magnetic state, as sympathy, thought-reading and clairvoyance, without becoming unconscious in the least, but continuing in a condition of full wakefulness. If the sleep occurs, as it sometimes will in very susceptible subjects, before the physician is aware of it, it is not to be deemed an obstacle to a cure. It must be turned to a good account. It is better that they be allowed to remain in it from fifteen to thirty minutes before they are brought out of it. Give them the same treatment as you would if they were awake.

It is only necessary that the patient be thrown into the *impressible conscious state*. The sleep is useful only so far as it increases the susceptibility of the subject to your psychological influence. If the patient be one who is quite susceptible to the magnetic influence, which is the case with a considerable portion of chronic invalids, you can proceed at once to give him treatment without any preliminary process. If you have doubt of this, you can test his sensitiveness, if it is deemed desirable. Pass the hand or the points of the fingers, without contact, but very near, down the arm and over the palms of the hand of the patient, at the same time directing your mental force by intense gazing upon the parts, and, if susceptible, he will become conscious of a peculiar sensation, either that of a cool breeze, which is the most common, or a sense of warmth, or a prickling feeling, similar to that in the foot when it is going to sleep as it is called, or there will be a slight numbness. The more sensitive the subject of the experiment, the more vivid will be these sensations.

A diseased condition of the organism is often of itself a susceptible state. Deleutze, who never magnetized any but the sick, supposed that perfect health was an insusceptible condition. This was a conclusion not warranted, and is known now to be an error, yet there is no doubt the presence of a diseased condition renders one increasingly sensitive to all psychological influences, which is a hint of nature poining to magnetism as the divine method of cure.

It may be laid down as an axiom that, in order to the production of the highest curative results, the state of unconscious coma is by no means an essential prerequisite, but only a conscious *impressible state*, in which the will of the operator and the simplest suggestion from him becomes the highest law of the patient's being, and a spiritual force adequate to control all his sensations, his voluntary muscular motions, the action of the involuntary organic functions, and his mental states. In this condition the mind and will of the physician, acting in harmony with the yielding and accordant mind and will of the patient, triumph over the diseased condition of the latter. Every disease, if of a nature, and in such a stage, as to admit of a cure, surrenders to this psychological force as to its lawful sovereign.

It has long been known that a person can be thrown into a state where all his voluntary motions are under the control of another. If the hand be closed, and he be told that he cannot open it, he finds it impossible to do so, though all the time perfectly wakeful and conscious. He cannot do it, simply because he believes he cannot, and does not, and perhaps cannot, will it, or, to use a common form of expression of subjects in this state, he does not *wish* to do it. He has unresistingly delivered himself to the control of another. His will and affections consent to this bondage. If he be told that he cannot raise his hand to his head, he finds that he cannot, though he may seem to struggle hard to accomplish it. The effort is wholly external, while internally he does not desire it or will it. If the hand be placed upon the head, and you *suggest* to him that he cannot remove it, he finds himself without the power to do it, though he may appear to struggle hard to do so, until the magnetizer pronounces the words, " All right," or, "Now you can;" then he does it with ease. In the same way, he cannot walk across the room, nor even speak his own name, if the despotic will of the person into whose care the subject has delivered himself *suggest* that he cannot. All his sensations, as well as his muscular movements, are under the control of the magnetizer. He can be made to feel warm or cold, hungry or thirsty, to see, hear, smell, taste, or feel anything, and to feel sick or well. He can be thrown into any mental state you may wish to induce upon him. You can make him feel joyful or sad, humble or proud, devotional or the contrary, hopeful or despairing, benevolent or selfish. It is also a fact of great value, *that the silent suggestion of the operator, or his simple will, without any vocal expression, will act with equal force, when the state is fully established.*

Here seems to be a power that is adequate to cure disease, and when so used finds its legitimate employment. I have applied it to that purpose, and to that alone, never using it for the exhibition of any of the other phenomena. The psychopathic physician, whom God and the angel-world have called to the sublime mission of healing the sick and relieving human suffering, should never degrade it, and abuse it, by putting it to any inferior use. Some of the public exhibitions of it, under the name of psychology or biology, have been simply ridiculous, and calculated to fill every sensible mind with disgust. It has had much to do in bringing it into disrepute, and repelled the scientific physician from its employment as a remedial agency. But so wonderful a power may find its legitimate sphere of use. There cannot be the shadow of a doubt of its efficiency and value as a therapeutic agency. If it be a fact, that in this form of the magnetic state you can gain an almost absolute control over all the voluntary muscular movements, and even the sensations of the patient, why may you not just as well and as certainly affect the physiological action of the involuntary organs? Such I know, by hundreds of successful experiments, continued through many years, to be the truth. In the case of a susceptible patient, your simple suggestion, made in the silent depth of your own consciousness, or ultimated in vocal language, becomes a word of power, and can increase or diminish the action of the heart, change the character of the respiration, affect, in any desirable way, the functional movements of the stomach, the liver, the kidneys, and the intestinal canal. You can affect in a moment the action of the perspiratory glands, and throw the patient into a gentle sweat. You can control the vital action of any organ of the body, render any part insensible to pain, and calm the excited nerves, and, in a word, produce the specific effects of any medicine that was ever administered, without any of the usual reactive morbid results. If this is true of this wonderful agent, — and it is among the certainties that it is true, — what medicine under heaven can be found which is so immediate and potent in its effects? Here we witness the sovereignty of mind over matter. For it is the divine order and the law of creation, that the spiritual should govern the material — that the whole realm of matter should be under the dominion of the world of spirit.

But the question will naturally arise, Can these effects be made permanent? It seems to be a general impression among physicians and others, who may admit the immediate beneficial effects of the psychopathic treatment, that they are transient, and will only last for a few days at most. If this be so, what then? When a physician gives morphine or bromide of potassium, or gelseminum, or chloral hydrate, to a nervous invalid, does he expect that its influence will last forever? What course then does he take when the effects of the medicine are seen to be temporary, and have all disappeared? After a proper interval, he administers another dose. So let us follow up the psychopathic treatment, until the organism of the patient undergoes a radical and permanent change, and a complete revolution is effected in the organic functions. If, in our first attack upon the disease, we gain any advantage, follow it up until the invader is expelled. But experiment has proved that the effects which are produced upon the patient while in the conscious impressible state, he may be made to carry over into his normal condition. If the operator and the patient suppose that the effects will be transient, they will be so; for the law holds good here, if nowhere else, "Be it unto thee according to thy faith." If they both combine to will and believe that they will be permanent, such will be the result. In the impressible state, the patient comes under the action of the law of faith, the great psychological remedy in the Gospel system, the importance of which even the Christian world has never fully appreciated. But the life of Jesus, the Christ, has affixed to it the divine seal, and demonstrated to all future ages that it is one of the highest laws of our being and the divine mode of cure.

CHAPTER V.

HOW TO INDUCE THE IMPRESSIBLE STATE.

The First Aim of the Physician — The State easily Induced — Freedom from Disturbing Influences — Position of the Patient — Reasons for it — Effect of Gazing — Fascination — Use of the Hands — State of the Cerebrum in the Somnambulic Condition — The Cerebellum — Control of the Voluntary and Involuntary Functions — Influence of the Patient's Mind — Sensitiveness to Psychological Force — The Origin of Disease — Word of Power — Influence of Suggestion in the Normal State — Spiritual Forces and Material Effects — Ever Present.

IF the effects described in the preceding chapter can be produced upon the sensitive subject, it becomes a question of great practical value, How can the *impressible conscious state* be induced, in which the mental force of the physician, combined with that of the invalid, can affect the physiological action of every organ of the body? Where it is not the normal state of the patient, it must be the first aim of the physician to produce it, to some extent at least, as his success will depend upon the degree in which it exists, and little can be done without it. In certain cases both time and patience may be requisite. It is highly probable that, under the proper conditions, all persons may be brought into it. To a greater extent than is generally believed it is a self-induced condition, and the physician is only an assistant in its production. The state is one of perfect passivity, intense mental concentration and abstraction.

There should be perfect stillness, and freedom from everything that can distract the mind. All conversation must be suspended. There must be a mutual co-operation of the physician and patient. The latter must be entirely passive and yield himself wholly to the former. Let the subject assume an easy position, so that all the voluntary muscles may be relaxed. Though it is not absolutely necessary, yet it is important, that he sit with his back toward the north, and in a somewhat reclining posture. There is no doubt that the magnetism of the earth has a polar distribution. It is equally certain that the odyllic emanation of the terrestrial magnet has also a polar arrangement. It was the opinion of Reichenbach, with which some other scientific men concur, that the Aurora Borealis and Aurora Australis are the odylic light of the north and south poles. There are some persons so extremely sensitive to the magnetic influence that they cannot sleep at night unless the head lies toward the north, so as to bring the body into harmony with the poles of the earth. In any other position they are uneasy, wakeful, and restless. Children sometimes in their sleep turn around spontaneously without waking. I am satisfied that this is not the effect of imagination, as many persons have discovered it from their own experience, who could give no reason why it was so, and who knew nothing of magnetism. A bar of iron, set up at an angle of forty-five degrees, with one end leaning toward the north, will become temporarily magnetic. The lower end will be found, on testing it, to be the north pole, and the upper end the south pole. The patient should be caused, in harmony with this law, to sit or recline with the back toward the north. This will increase his susceptibility to the psychic influence, and tend to invert the magnetic poles of the body.

The brain, which is normally positive, or the north pole of the body, will become negative, and its magnetism will flow downward toward the feet.

The assistant must aim to produce only the conscious impressible state, as this is all that is necessary to the cure of disease. The patient may be informed of your intention or not, as your judgment may decide to be expedient. Let the subject gaze intently at some object held a little above and before the eyes, so as to strain the eye upward while looking at it. It is not a matter of much importance what the object is, as it is not probable that it has any direct electric action, as some have supposed, but only assists the patient to concentrate his mind and throw him into the passive state. It may be held in the hand, in which case it becomes charged with your psychic and odyllic force; or it may be suspended from the wall of the room. I use for the purpose a small silver cross. A coin, or the knob of a pencil-case, will answer equally well. At the same time that the subject is looking steadily at this, let the assistant gaze intensely at the same or at the patient's forehead. This will increase the effect, as the magnetism of the eye, through which the mind acts or goes forth, is of equal efficiency with that of the hand. Fascination or charming is affected by gazing at the object. Animals of prey, as the cat, fix their victims by gazing at them before they spring upon them. You see this in the cat when catching a bird or a fly. Avail yourself of this hint. Concentrate your whole mental force into the act of gazing. Only a few minutes, scarcely ever more than five, will be necessary to produce the impressible state, in which the patient will become sensitive to your psychological force, and *suggestion* will act as a controlling power.

After gazing for a few minutes, in the manner above described, gently place your hands, one on the forebrain and the other on the cerebellum, or the back of the head and neck, at the same time willing the vital force of the cerebrum to retreat backward to the cerebellum. This is the physiological condition of the brain in the somnambulic state and in ordinary sleep. The cerebrum, or large brain, is the organ of the mind in a state of wakefulness, and of our voluntary life and activity. The cerebellum is the organ of our involuntary life. Gazing with the eyes partly shut, or with a sort of double squint, at an object elevated about forty-five degrees above the eyes, tends to invert and suspend the action of the large brain, and throw it into a quiescent state. When this is accomplished, you will find that your control of the patient is completely established. What you say to him is the law of his being. You hold the key of his very life. You can render him insensible to pain in any part, by a simple suggestion, and when he is restored to the normal state the diseased part may be left insensible. You can allay inflammation in any organ, or infuse spiritual force and strength into any weakened part. In a word, you can produce any desired effect. If the control is not completely established, the process to which the patient has submitted will greatly increase his susceptibility to the sanative influence of the psychopathic treatment.

In this state, he must be made to *forget* his disease. When persons are fully magnetized and thrown into the somnambulic state, they can be made to remember or to forget anything which occurs in that state. If you will them to remember, they will remember. If you tell them to forget anything or everything, they will be unable to recollect. They will be like one who is conscious of having dreamed in his sleep, but cannot recall his dream. So the patient must be made to forget his disease, and to abstract his mind from it. And your success in curing him will depend, to a great extent, upon your skill in managing and controlling his mind. In all systems of medicine the mind has much to do in the cure of disease. Most diseases originate in disturbed mental and spiritual states. In the impressible state the mind acts with increased force, — with tenfold energy. In an instant, it can create disease and pain in any part, or it can render any part insensible to pain and create health. Your simple word, acting in concert with the consenting will of the subject, seems to be endowed with creative force. It becomes an image of the eternal Logos, the Word that was in the beginning with God, and was God, and by which all things were created. You speak, and it is done. You command, and it stands fast. So potential a sanative agency is not found in the whole realm of nature.

Since many persons, and perhaps all, may be brought into the impressible conscious state, while only a few are good subjects for the exhibition of the somnambulic sleep, we see the great value of this process in the cure of disease. For it is certain that the sleep alone is of little or no importance. Its value depends upon the impressibility of the patient while in the sleep, and is measured by the degree in which that susceptibility exists. When we see a person in a state so sensitive to the action of the mind of another, though perfectly conscious of everything that transpires around him, and to all outward appearance in his natural state of wakefulness, that by a simple suggestion, an arm may be rendered insensible to the otherwise severest pain, and the action of any organ may be affected in any desired way, we cannot for a moment doubt the practical remedial value of such a power. And it is no honor to a physician's head or heart, who obstinately remains ignorant of so potent a therapeutic agent, and who utterly discards its use. The time is not far distant when its value will be understood and generally recognized, and the laws by which it is governed will be studied. No course of medical education will be deemed complete without it. The time is at hand when it will be as discreditable for a physician to be ignorant of the science of Medical Psychology, as it would now be for him to be without a knowledge of physiology and chemistry.

The force of suggestion, as it is called by the late Dr. Gregory, in the natural state, has long been known. Many interesting facts illustrating its influence are familiar to all. The simple remark, made by another, that an invalid looks worse and appears to be running down, will have its effect in helping along his decline. And the suggestion that a patient looks better, and appears to be improving, will have its influence in the direction of health. But in the impressible state suggestion acts with a hundred-fold force. In this lies its great value as a curative agency. The cures effected by it are accomplished by spiritual forces, which are none the less potential for being invisible. All causes are unseen. The whole material universe is the region of effects; the spiritual world is the realm of causation. If I raise my hand to my head, or strike a blow with my arm, the visible motion is an effect, but my mind and will are the unseen and spiritual force that is the cause. But it is equally true that all causes are spiritual and invisible. In our ordinary state, our senses are limited to the cognizance of visible effects, while the unseen forces are concealed from view. In that state of mental exaltation and freedom from material thraldom, which has received the name of clairvoyance, and also in the spiritual world, to which our inner life belongs, "the invisible appears in sight," and the mind is elevated to the perception of the hidden causes of things. The mind is taken behind the curtain, and sees the now invisible forces that move the sublime machinery of nature, and which are the secret spring of its life and activity. Psychopathy owes much of its efficiency as a remedial agent to its relationship to the invisible and potent active forces of the universe, and especially those that impel the organic machinery of the human body. It brings the mind into its divinely appointed relation to matter as its controlling, governing principle, and man takes his proper place at the head of creation, as its lawful sovereign.

EVER PRESENT.

" The sun of yesterday is set —
 Forever set to Time and me;
Yet of its warmth, and of its light,
 Something I feel and something see.

" The flower of yesterday is not —
 Its faded leaves are scattered wide;
Yet of its perfume do I breathe,
 Still does its beauty stir my pride.

" The friend of yesterday is dead —
 On yonder hill his grave doth lie;
Yet there are moments when I feel
 His presence, as of old, draw nigh.

" A part of what has been remains;
 The essences of what is gone
Are ever present to my sense;
 Though left, I am not left forlorn.

"In thought, in feeling, and in love,
  Things do not perish, though they pass;
The form is shattered to the eye,
  But only broken is the glass.

"Sun, friend, and flower have each become
  A part of my immortal part;
They are not lost, but evermore
  Shine, live, and bloom within my heart."

CHAPTER VI.

MEDICAL PSYCHOLOGY AND THE LIMITATIONS TO ITS ABUSE

Drugs may be Abused — Illustrations — Chloroform — Special Guards against the Perversion of the Agent in Psychopathy — The State Voluntary — An Evil Design a Loss of Power — Quickens the Intuitions — Difficulty of Deception — Relative Strength of Good and Evil — Exaltation of the Moral Sense — Magnetism as a Reformative Influence — Refinement of the Character — Quotation from Dr. Gregory — Influence of Mind on Mind — Swedenborg's Theory of Disease — A Medical Psycholgy Practicable — Dr. C. F. Taylor — Bichat on the Influence of the Emotions on Organic Life.

IT may be asked, "Is it proper for one person to subject himself so completely to the control of another? Could not such a power be perverted to purposes of evil?"

I am convinced that the state described in the previous chapter has been generally misunderstood. It is not so much the absolute control of one person by some mysterious power in another, as it is a restoration of the subject to self-control, and the complete dominion of the higher over the lower nature in man, which is the divine order of human existence. In most invalids the sceptre has been wrested from the sovereign mind, and by a disorderly revolution usurped by the body and the external spiritual nature. In the psychopathic treatment we aim to restore the dethroned dynasty of the mind, and reinstate the spiritual powers in their lawful sovereignty.

The practitioners of Medical Psychology, if they understand their proper function and use, only assist the invalid to gain this desirable end. It is not so much their aim to make an ostentatious display of their own psychological powers, as to emancipate and bring into activity the imprisoned and dormant forces of the patient's own mind. Their mental and will force is only auxiliary to that of his. They assist to break his chains, and end the unnatural bondage of his higher to his lower nature, and of the internal to the external. As the body without the spirit is dead, the soul, with its godlike powers, is the divinely appointed monarch of the whole physiological domain. The physician's mind is an ally of that of the invalid; this is his appropriate office.

I am not aware that there is any greater confidence necessary to be placed in the psychopathic physician than must be reposed in the ordinary practitioner of medicine. It might be equally proper to inquire if the poisonous drugs, employed as remedies in disease, could not be easily abused? An over-dose of strychnia, or belladonna, or veratrum, would be attended with fatal results. It would be easy to give a man morphine enough, not merely to quiet his pain, but to extinguish his life. This has been done, both by accident and design. Serious charges have been made by patients of evil treatment at the hands of dentists, and other doctors, while the victims were unconscious, under the influence of anæsthetic agents. But, whether true or false, they constitute no valid objection against their legitimate employment. Chloroform may be used to render the subject of a surgical operation insensible to pain, which is its proper use, or it may be employed to aid in robbery and plunder. It is a universal law that everything good may be perverted to an evil use. But the power by which one mind appears to control the mental manifestations and physical functions of another seems to have been, in an especial manner, guarded, by the Author of nature, against abuse. In the first place, the surrender of the subject passively to the influence of the physician is entirely voluntary, and the continuance of his psychological control is at any and every moment at the consent of the patient. It can be thrown off at any time, and in a moment, if the subject sees reason to do so. If anything occurs demanding it, he can assert his freedom, and end his bondage at once, which is always more apparent than real. The state is as voluntary in its continuance as in its commencement.

Again, it is not only impossible to acquire control over a patient without his consent, but no one can gain, by mere psychic force, a complete ascendency over another person for an evil purpose. The evil design and the predominant action of the lower propensities, in one base enough to attempt it, render him negative, and deprive him of power to magnetize at all, especially one in whom the higher intellectual and moral nature is predominant. Even if he should succeed in inducing the impressible state in any degree, it quickens the intuitive perceptions of the patient, and his design is detected at once. He is placing his intended victim in an exalted intellectual position, where deception becomes impossible. No person who is not already confirmed in the love of evil can be psychologically controlled for any improper object. No one who was not already corrupt was ever corrupted by it. A state of moral and intellectual elevation is always psychologically superior to a lower spiritual condition. Evil may be overcome with good, for this is the divine order. But goodness is more than a match for depravity in all its forms.

Again, no one at all acquainted with the phenomena of what is called the magnetic state can have failed to notice, as one of its most obvious effects, that it greatly quickens the *moral sensibilities* of the patient. Its influence here is of equal if not of greater value than its physiological effects. It has its high moral uses, when properly understood and employed, as a reformatory and restorative agency, as well as in the cure of disease. A person no sooner enters the state than he experiences a marked exaltation of his whole intellectual and moral nature. Individuals having the reputation of being morally depraved seem to be elevated by it to a higher spiritual level, and make an approach to the saintly character. If we were capable of trying to persuade the magnetized person to a bad action, or to consent to any evil practice whatever, we should soon discover that his sense of moral obligation has been quickened to a degree not exhibited by the same person in the normal state. Sometimes, and usually, the countenance becomes more refined in its expression, and the tone of the voice is changed, indicating externally the higher tone of moral feeling. They seem ardently to love truth, and it is well-nigh impossible to make them say what they deem an untruth. They may be deceived, but they will not lie. All the moral powers seem equally exalted in their action. As Dr. Gregory remarks: "Their whole manner seems to undergo a refinement, which, in the higher stages of the magnetic state, reaches a most striking point, insomuch that we see, as it were, before us, persons of a much more elevated character than the same individuals seem to be when awake. It would seem as if the lower animal propensities were laid to rest, while the intellect and higher sentiments shone forth with a lustre that is undiminished by aught that is mean or common."

Though in the psychopathic treatment we never aim to produce the state of coma, or the complete magnetic condition, but only the impressible conscious state, yet we affirm that similar moral and spiritual effects result from it. We do not seek to gain dominion over an invalid, but to restore him to true freedom, the government of himself in its fullest sense. We do not know but that, in common with everything else, it may in some degree be abused, but we affirm that God has hedged it round with such protective limitations and laws as to render its abuse more difficult than almost any other agency.

It is an established fact, as well demonstrated as any principle in the philosophy of mind, that every person is influenced by the presence of others, and persons of heightened nervous sensibility in a marked degree. Mind acts on mind, as certainly as all matter in the universe is connected by the law of gravitation. There is great reality in this invisible but often potent spiritual influence, going forth with the emanating sphere of our inner nature. It is in consequence of this that two silent persons find themselves occupied with the same line of thought at the same time, and that we often have an indefinable perception, more or less vivid, of the near approach of some intimate acquaintance and friend. By the same law we imbibe, in spite of all our volitions, the prevailing feelings of those who are around us. In the psychopathic treatment of mental and physical disorders, we accept this inevitable fact of mutual influence, and only aim to place the patient in a condition in which this law is intensified in its operation, and more marked in its beneficent results.

In harmony with this law of the action of mind on mind, invalids, especially those of great nervous impressibility, become subject to the disturbing influence of disorderly spirits, which aggravates their morbid condition. Swedenborg taught a century ago that disease has a correspondence with disordered mind in the other realm of being and a spiritual origin. (Arcana Celestia, 5711-5727.) This is not recognized in the modern materialistic systems of pathological science, but is a prominent feature in the medical system of the New Testament, and was recognized as true by the Great Physician. To cure disease and to cast out demons, or to release the patient from a disorderly psychological influence and control, are in the Gospels equivalent expressions. Certain diseases, as chorea, paralysis, and epilepsy, are attributed to a spiritual origin; but these peculiar nervous and cerebral disorders can with no more show of reason be ascribed to this cause than many others to which mankind are subject. If this is true,— and the progressive medical science of the New Age which has come to the dawn is beginning cautiously to admit it, — then there can be such a thing as a genuine and efficient system of Medical Psychology, for we are told, in the spiritual philosophy of the Scandinavian Seer, that every change in our mental and spiritual status modifies our relation to and connection with the intelligences, good or evil, of the other sphere of life. The mental condition of a patient must therefore be a matter of no secondary importance, both as it concerns his connection with the world of spirits and its influence, but also in its immediate effect upon the organic system and its dynamic forces. The influence of the mind upon the body, for good or ill, is far more immediate and marked than that of any chemical combinations that can be administered.

On this important but too often neglected subject, Dr. C. F. Taylor, in his Theory and Practice of the Movement Cure, remarks: "The special influence of the mind and will upon the general bodily nutrition is daily manifested and acknowledged by every physician. Each mental manifestation has its ultimation somewhere in the bodily organism, its natural language of position and motion peculiar to itself, thus affecting of course the nutrition of the muscular tissue employed in maintaining that position, but when the mental states are of a disordered and depressing character, they occasion more or less disturbance of the functions and their physiological processes."

Bichat, for many years a reigning authority in physiololgy, speaks of the positive and immediate effects of the emotions and passions upon the organic system. He says: "Strict observation proves to us that the parts subservient to the internal functions are constantly affected by them, and are ever determined according to the state in which they may be. The effect of every kind of passion is to produce some change, some alteration in organic life. Anger accelerates the circulation, and increases, often in an incommensurable proportion, the effort of the heart; it is on the force, the rapidity of the course of the blood that it maintains its influence. Joy affects the circulation also, but without producing so sensible a change; it develops its phenomena in greater plentitude, accelerates it gently, and determines it toward the surface. Fear acts in an inverse ratio; it is characterized by a feebleness in the whole vascular system,—a feebleness which, preventing the arrival of the blood to the capillaries, produces that general paleness, which is observed in the body, and particularly in the face. The effect of sadness and trouble is somewhat similar.

"Respiration has a no less immediate dependence on the passions; those suffocations, that oppression, the sudden effect of profound grief, do they not indicate some remarkable change, some sudden alteration in the lungs? In the long catalogue of chronic diseases, or of acute affections, the sad attribute of the pulmonary system, are we not often obliged to trace the different passions of the patient to discover the principle of his disease?" In another chapter he shows the influence of the mental states upon the voluntary and involuntary muscular system. (*Physiological Researches upon Life and Death*, pp. 45, 46.)

All this proves that if it be found practicable to control or influence the mental manifestations of an invalid, there can be a Medical Psychology. For as both general and local effects are produced by the variations of the mental states, so these by the psychopathic physician may be directed to the accomplishment of special purposes, and thus exhibit the action of mental medicine. There is a pathology of the mind as well as of the body, and these sustain to each other a correspondent or causal relation. The one is prior, the other posterior. The mental disturbance is the hidden cause of the bodily malady, which is only an effect. A true medical system must carry its curative agencies into the realm of causation. One of the improvements of modern medical science is found in its more thorough search into the causes of disease. This is turning the attention in the right direction in order to the discovery of the most efficient curative agencies and appliances.

CHAPTER VII.

AUTO-MAGNETISM; OR, SELF-HEALING.

Self-magnetization Practicable — Professional Seers — Spontaneous Somnambulism — The Essential Thing — How to Induce the State — Passes Unnecessary — Method of Mr. Braid — How the Condition may be Self-induced — Oriental Method — Natural Sleep — Directions to be followed in Auto-magnetism — How to become Mentally Perceptive — Transference of the Senses — Psychometry — Philosophy of Self-healing — Susceptibility of the Body to Mental Influences — How to Relieve yourself of Pain — Also of Disease — How to make a Weakened Organ Strong — The Way to Increase Vital Action — How to change our Mental States — Mental Contrasts.

IF any one cannot find a person in whom he has sufficient confidence to entrust himself to his care in the interior impressible state, or, for any reason, a good assistant is not at hand, and no foreign aid is available, he may be taught how to induce it in himself. Self-magnetization, with proper instruction, is easily practised. The patient's own mind has always much to do in producing the impressible state, and even the sleep. Thousands of persons, without any assistance from others, throw themselves into the somnambulic condition of the brain. It is witnessed every day, and in all parts of the country. We have seen hundreds of persons who could induce upon themselves the conscious magnetic state in a few minutes. Some can go into it almost instantly, and with some it has become well-nigh a normal and permanent condition. Many professional clairvoyants throw themselves into a state of artificial somnambulism in a minute, and bring themselves out of it at pleasure. This proves that the state is under the control of the will, and may be self-induced, if we acquire a knowledge of its nature and the laws governing it. The frequent occurrence of natural or spontaneous somnambulism, which is identical with the magnetic sleep, proves that it arises from some power or cause residing within the system of the subject. If so, it is not unreasonable to suppose, that, like ordinary sleep, it may, by following the right course, be voluntarily induced. The more it is practised, the easier it becomes. Any one can readily put himself into the *impressible conscious state*, which is all that is requisite to the practice of self-healing.

Let it be remembered that the essential thing, in the magnetic or impressible condition, is the quiescence of the large brain, and the suspension of its vital activity. When this is the case, the consciousness, and all the mental functions of thought and sensation, are performed by the cerebellum, or little brain, which is the organ of the involuntary life. This becomes the organ by which we think, will, and act. It is a state of extreme sensitiveness to mental impressions, whether arising from within ourselves or from others. But how can this change be effected, and this transference of the vital force from one department of the cerebral structure to the other, be accomplished? Mr. Braid, of Manchester, England, a successful and distinguished practitioner of magnetism, under the name of hypnotism, appears to have been among the first who doubted the necessity of any influence foreign to the patient, in order to induce the magnetic state, with all its characteristic phenomena. It has been found that gazing steadily at an object, held a little above the eyes, and in front of the upper part of the forehead, will induce the state, without the use of the prescribed passes that have continued to be used from the time of Mesmer downward. By gazing in this strained position, necessitating the rolling up of the eye, the action of the cerebrum is soon suspended, and the passive impressible state, which is only an introverted condition of the mind, is induced. This position of the eye would effect the same, without gazing at anything, but it might be more difficult for some in this way to control the attention. Now all this one can do alone, although I am not prepared to say that the presence and influence of a good assistant might not facilitate the process, especially before one has become accustomed to it. The method of inducing interior perception, long practised by the magicians of the East, was by gazing at an ink-spot. Steadily looking at some small object or figure on the ceiling of the bedroom, will induce sleep, when a person is inclined to wakefulness. This I have often tried with success. The sleep in this case may be partly somnambulic, but is extremely tranquil and refreshing. The late Dr. Gregory gives the same testimony, from his own experience, regarding it.

As previously directed, in the instructions given respecting the induction of the interior sensitive state by another, let the patient assume an easy position, and be quiet and passive. A recumbent posture is a good one. Then direct the attention to some object, so situated as to require the eyes to be somewhat elevated in order to see it. Abstract the attention from everything else, and gaze steadily at it, with the eyes partly closed, for a few moments. As soon as the eyes feel a tendency to close entirely, and the room seems dark, or the vision blurred and obscure, shut them at once.

Continue to gaze mentally at the same object, after the eyes are closed, and you will find that you can see it nearly as well as before. This is an interior vision, and the dawning of spiritual perception or vision independent of the external organs of sight. Continue perfectly passive and quiet. You are now in the state of sleep-waking, and on the boundary of both worlds. It is a condition of mental exaltation, of quickened perceptions, and great psychological sensitiveness. If it is your wish to become mentally perceptive, direct your thoughts to some distant and familiar object or person, or to some place where you would *love* to be. You will perceive objects with the interior eye, as certainly and as really as you ever saw them with the outward organ. You will perceive not only what you have seen before, but what now exists, though you never before saw it. The accuracy of this you may be able to test, if you desire it. I have done it many times, and found it as reliable as our ordinary vision. While in this state, you can, by an effort of will, transfer the interior sense of vision to any distance,—even to another continent. For this wonderful power is not subject to the limitations of time or space. It is not imagination merely,—it is a real interior or spiritual perception. The power we call imagination may be, and without doubt often is, an inward seeing. All the senses may act independently of their material organs, and be transferred to any distance. By fixing the attention upon the organ of hearing, and listening, you can sometimes hear what persons, many miles away, are saying. The sound is distinctly heard, though not with the outward ear. In fact, incredible as it may appear, their very thoughts become audible. This has been called *clairaudience.* The same is true of the sense of smell, and even taste.

It is only the mind asserting its freedom from material restraint. A little practice, and a due share of perseverance, will render all this easy, and you will be able to enter upon this state without any preliminary process of gazing. Some, undoubtedly, will succeed better than others; but no one need fail entirely.

While in this state, if you turn your attention to any persons at a distance, or near by you, by closely watching your sensations, you will find that their states, bodily and mental, will affect you. If they are sad, you will *feel* it. If they have a pain, you will be affected with it by sympathy, in the same place, and in a perceptible degree. By holding in your hand an autograph letter from a person, many miles away, you will be influenced by his states, and will have an indescribable perception also of him and his surroundings, and even his past history and character. This is sympathetic clairvoyance or psychometry. By means of it you will be able after a while to tell the condition of your absent friends and others, though they may be thousands of miles distant. In this state all the senses are reduced to a unity, — an indefinable inward perceptivity.

You are now in the impressible state. The body and all its organs are extremely sensitive to mental influences, either from yourself or others. Your disease will be found, to a great extent, under your own control. Your silent suggestion will now be a spiritual force that will influence the physiological action of the various organs. If you imagine a pain in any part, you will feel it more or less, according to the degree of your sensitiveness. If your head aches, suggest to yourself that it is gone or is leaving you, at the same time calmly willing it to depart, and it will be instantly relieved. If your feet are cold, and consequently the opposite pole of the body hot and pressed with blood and the nerve force, suggest to yourself that they are becoming warm, and you will be astonished to perceive how soon they will begin to glow with heat. Whatever you suggest, and will, and *believe*, is at once done. The body obeys the slightest hint from the sovereign mind. The mind is restored to its lawful sovereignty, and asserts its divine right to rule the whole physiological domain. It governs its own material world *dei gratia*, by the grace of God. If you will any change to be effected, and *believe* it, it is certain to be so, for the whole system now comes under the action of the law of faith. What some call imagination or fancy becomes at once a reality. This strange power becomes an actual creative force. Faith operates with greater power. If you are afflicted with any pain or disease, understanding as you now do that it is one of the laws of our being, that while in this susceptible state the body is subject to the mind, it ought to be no more difficult to believe that you will feel better of your disease, than to give credence to the proposition that the sun will rise to-morrow morning. It is not mere fancy any more than your disease is. You are not called to the exercise of a blind faith, but an intelligent confidence in the operation of the divine laws of nature.

If there is pain or inflammation in any part, it is at once relieved by withdrawing the mind from it, and keeping the attention away from it. The diseased condition may be caused by an excessive accumulation and determination of the spiritual principle to the parts. The more perfectly you can abstract the mind from it, the greater will be the insensibility, and the more complete the relief. The pain is not in the material body, but in the spiritual organism. All sensation is in the mind. Withdraw this from the diseased part, and the pain and disease go with it. This can be done, for the spiritual element or principle is subject to your own will. It is well known that, in a revery, a person may even burn his hand, and not feel it. The part is virtually asleep. He is not sensible of pain until the attention is directed to it. In sleep all pains are unperceived; they are annihilated. We can learn to put any diseased and painful part to sleep by abstracting the mind and the consciousness from it, and thus leave the forces of nature to operate without obstruction and without interference. This alone will suffice to cure many forms of chronic disease. Here is a principle of great practical value, and one that will well repay patient study and thorough investigation.

If there be any part of the body in an opposite condition, that is, where the pathological state consists in weakness, diminished sensibility, coldness, or a lack of vitality, pursue a different course with it. Instead of abstracting the mind from it, infuse spiritual life into it. Turn the course of the vital current towards it, by directing the attention, the thoughts, and the will to it. It will be found more efficient than all stimulants, tonics, or liniments that were ever used.*
Give it large doses of spiritual medicine, for it is the spiritual element and force that it needs. You may say the blood does not flow to the weakened part or organ. That may be true. The nerves distributed to the place may be torpid, both those of sensation and of motion. But the real question is, What is the cause of this want of action in the vascular system, this torpidity, this

---

* The influence of *directed consciousness*, or the concentration of the attention, on the various bodily organs, is ably discussed in Dr. Holland's Mental Physiology, pp. 13–45.

weakened movement? It lacks the spiritual force, the living, moving principle. This lies at the root of the trouble. The remedy is to turn the vital stream in that direction. If there is a lack of life in any part, there is an excess of it somewhere else. Take from the one, and give to the other, and thus restore the balance. The restoration of the lost harmony is health. If we better understood the laws of our being, the relation of the mind to the body, the influence of the one upon the other both in health and disease, and the wonderful powers that are latent and dormant within us from not knowing how to use them, a physician would seldom be necessary. We should then possess the art of self-healing, and not often be under the necessity of going out of ourselves for the appropriate remedy for our diseases.

In changing the disordered mental states, as melancholy, anxiety, impatience, and despair, which lie at the root of most chronic ailments, we shall find it easy to do so in the self-induced impressible condition, if we voluntarily assume that attitude of body and expression of the face which the feelings or emotions we wish to excite cause us naturally to assume, and then they spontaneously arise within us. This is governed by a law of our nature, well stated by Maudsley: "When we put ourselves in the attitude that any passion naturally occasions, it is most certain that we acquire in some degree that passion. In our emotional life, any particular passion is rendered stronger and more distinct by the existence of those bodily states which it naturally produces, and which in turn, when otherwise produced, tend to engender it. Mr. Braid found, by experiments on persons whom he had put into a state of *hypnotism*, that by inducing attitudes of body natural to certain passions, he could excite those passions." (*Physiology and Pathology of the Mind*, p. 140.) Thus, if we place the face and limbs in an attitude which is the normal outward expression or correspondence of a certain emotion, that mental state will be actually excited. This subject has been fully discussed and illustrated in the previous work of the author, and it is necessary only to refer to it here. It is a principle of great practical value in the treatment of all chronic disturbances of the mental equilibrium and their corresponding morbid conditions of the physical organism.

There seems to be, as was noticed by Aristotle and Thomas Aquinas, a sort of antagonism or contrast in the affections of the mind, although they are in intimate association. So that every psychical bane has its proper antidote. Thus anxiety is counterbalanced and neutralized by resignation; fear by faith, hope and courage; melancholy by cheerfulness; sorrow and grief by joy and gladness; anger by placidity and self-control; and morbid haste and hurry of spirits by calmness and tranquillity. By attentively studying the morbid effect of thought and passion, we might often effect a salutary influence by establishing a train of contrasts in the mind, in the same way that for a poison introduced into the stomach and circulation, we give the appropriate chemical antidote. There is many a patient, who could be radically cured by a week of calm, unalloyed happiness. This is the panacea for all disordered, depressing mental states and the morbid bodily condition arising from them. Spinoza has actually reduced all the passions and affections of the mind to three radical ones, namely, joy, sorrow, and desire. The first arises when we pass from an imperfect to a better state, the second when we pass from a higher to a lower, and desire expresses the interior character of the individual.

CONQUER AND REST.

"Why not learn to conquer sorrow?
   Why not learn to smile at pain?
Why should every stormy morrow
   Shroud our way in gloom again?

"Why not lift the soul immortal
   Up to its angelic height—
Bid it pass the radiant portal
   Of the world of faith and light?

"Oh! there is another being
   All about us, all above,
Hid from mortal sense or seeing,
   Save the nameless sense of love.

"Not the love that dies like roses,
   When the frost-fire scathes the sod,
But the eternal rest that closes
   Round the soul that dwells in God.

"Into this great habitation
   Never tear or sorrow came,
Oh! it is the new creation,
   God its light, his love its flame.

"Up, O soul! and dwell forever
   On this hidden glorious shore;
Chilled by cloud-shade never, never,
   Up, and dwell for evermore."

CHAPTER VIII.

PHRENO-MAGNETISM AND ITS USE IN MEDICAL PSYCHOLOGY.

Phreno-Magnetism Defined — The Brain the Organ of the Mind — Stimulation of the Organs by the Touch — The Philosophy of it — How the Patient can do it himself — Sensitiveness of the Brain to Mental Force — How to Increase the Action of the Cerebral Organs — Importance of the Mental States — Their Relation to Disease — The Way to Allay the Over-Excitement of an Organ — Mental Maladies and their Cure — Health and Happiness — My Psalm.

IT is found that many persons, while in the impressible state, and even in their normal condition, by simply touching with your fingers the different phrenological organs, will exhibit, in a heightened degree, the mental faculty or function of which those parts of the brain are the outward manifestation or correspondence. By touching or pointing the finger at benevolence, or veneration, or hope, or self-esteem, they immediately feel, and outwardly manifest, each of those sentiments. This is called Phreno-Magnetism. It is now generally admitted by physiologists, that the brain is the organ of the mind, and that the several faculties of the mind act by means of different parts of the brain. Admitting this, it would seem to be practicable to excite or to allay the activity of the several organs. The increased action of those parts of the cerebral mass, occasioned by touching them, may result from two distinct causes, either of which may be adequate to produce the phenomenon above described. The odyllic and psychic emanation of the hand may afford a stimulus to that particular part of the brain, and thus increase its vital activity. We know that when we place the hand upon any part of the body, the place of contact immediately exhibits an increased vascular action. This is indicated by the heightened glow of that point of the body. The same effect would evidently be produced upon the brain. Touch the organ you wish to excite, or any part of the brain whose activity you may desire to augment, and silently will or suggest that they feel happy, or calm, or strong, or hopeful, as the case may require, and it will have its effect in inspiring the proper mental state. The feelings which you thus induce may be transferred to the normal condition, for your mental and magnetic force will give a healthier tone to the organs. In this way a thorough *conversion* may be wrought in their mental and spiritual status. But the touch of the hand excites the organ to increased action in another way. It draws the attention of the patient to that part of the brain which is the point of contact. It thus causes a concentration of his mental force to it, and thus augments its activity when otherwise it would be dormant. But it is evident that a patient can do this himself. If there be any mental faculty or faculties that are not sufficiently active, and a correspondingly depressed state of the feelings, as of hope, or courage, or energy, and he wishes to stimulate them to greater activity, let him direct his attention to them, and this will afford them their natural stimulus. If he cannot do it otherwise, let him place his finger upon them, so as to point the mind and direct the spiritual force to them. Once excited, they will continue so until adequate causes render them torpid; for a body at rest, by its own inertia, continues at rest until some force sets it in motion; and a body in motion continues its movement until stopped by a force equal to that which originated its motion. There are some persons who can excite in themselves any organ of the brain they choose, and in a moment, and thus can give increased activity and intensity to any feeling or sentiment. If hope is in a negative or depressed state, and we are inclined to discouragement and despair, let us fix the attention upon that part of the cerebrum which is the organ of hope, and, if need be, place your finger upon it, and a joyful sunshine will light your darkness. The same may be said of mirthfulness, of firmness, of self-esteem, or any of the cerebral organs. The brain is singularly sensitive to mental force. By directing the mind to any part of it, and fixing the attention upon it, its vital activity is increased.

He who makes use of the psychopathic treatment for the cure of disease will always find it necessary to attend to the mental states of his patients. This is a matter of supreme importance, for in their disordered spiritual condition lies the root of their disease. Health and happiness are inseparably connected. No one can be well who is habitually under the influence of melancholy, or anxiety, or despair, or any of the depressing mental emotions. These must be removed before a healthy and harmonious action of the bodily organs can be established. It is one of the higher uses and advantages of medical psychology that it makes the patient happy in proportion as he comes under its influence. This alone is far better than any medicinal compounds. Cheerfulness, and a heart serenely blissful, have a sanative virtue and potency beyond that of the most powerful drug. The psychopathic physician must infuse into his patients, hope, faith, courage, energy, and contentment. In a word, he must make them tranquilly happy. This he will find it easy to do, by following out the hints given in this chapter, especially if he is himself under the dominion of those sentiments. He will easily communicate their spiritual contagion and the sphere of their influence to others, and impregnate them with his own happiness.

It is also in the power of any one, especially if assisted by a congenial and sympathetic friend, to allay or diminish the action of any organ in the brain, and put it, as it were, to sleep. Sometimes people find themselves in an unhappy, and consequently an unhealthy state, from the abnormal excitement of certain phrenological organs, and the feelings of which they are the exponent. Fear, in some of its multifarious forms, is too active. They are filled with baseless anxieties, and doubts, and forebodings; or combativeness is in a fever heat, so that they are impatient, morbidly sensitive, excitable, and irritable. Health is impossible in such a state of mind. To diminish the activity of any organ in the brain, pursue a course the opposite of that which is necessary to augment its movement and increase its excitement. While in the self-induced impressible state, turn the mental force and withdraw the spiritual principle from it. The withdrawal of all mental stimulus from it will quiet its abnormal excitement. The blood, the nervous force, and the magnetic life will no longer rush towards the part, but will be determined to other portions of the organism. It will assist in doing this if the physician places his hand upon the organ for a moment, and then removes it to the shoulders, or some point below. This produces a derivative effect. The magnetism, as it is called, imparted by the hand will be attracted downward, and the accumulated odyleic and nervous force of that part of the brain with it. The patient, of course, must co-operate with the physician in this cure of his mental maladies. He should be taught and empowered to have no regret for the past, or anxiety about the future. Learn him to live in the present moment, to find something to enjoy here and now, and not to feed his soul on the unsubstantial shadows of past enjoyments. We can never recall the past. When we find our only bliss in living over in our memory pleasant scenes and sacred joys that have gone by, our life stands still. We stay in our march of progression. It can afford, at most, only a painful pleasure, — the joy of grief. Our motto should be, Onward and upward. To think too much of past joys is to fail of realizing the good with which the present moment always comes freighted. Forgetting the things that are behind, we should reach forth unto those that are before. Whether we see it and believe it, or not, the gateway of a glorious future is opening before every human soul, and our pathway to-day is somehow leading to it. Then let hope spring eternal in the human breast, and let us find a perpetual feast of enjoyment in the divine arrangements of the present minute. In the calm contentment and serene happiness that accompany a life of unselfish activity and usefulness, we may attain the enduring bliss "that mixes man with heaven,". and gain a spiritual standing-ground, where the light from higher skies slips down and mingles with the blue of our own firmament, and we hear another and sweeter music through all of earth's harmonies.

MY PSALM.

"I mourn no more my vanished years;
Beneath a tender rain,
An April rain of smiles and tears,
My heart is young again.

" The west winds blow, and, singing low,
 I hear the glad streams run;
The windows of my soul I throw
 Wide open to the sun.

" No longer forward nor behind
 I look in hope or fear;
But, grateful, take the good I find,
 The best of now and here.

" I plough no more a barren land,
 To harvest weed and tare;
The manna dropping from God's hand
 Rebukes my painful care.

" I break my pilgrim staff, I lay
 Aside the toiling oar;
The angel sought so far away
 I welcome at my door.

" All as God wills, who wisely heeds
 To give or to withhold,
And knoweth more of all my needs
 Then all my prayers have told!

" Enough that blessings undeserved
 Have marked my erring track;
That whereso'er my feet have swerved,
 His chastening turned me back;

" That more and more a Providence
 Of Love is understood,
Making the springs of time and sense
 Sweet with eternal good;

" That death seems but a covered way
 That opens into light,
Wherein no blinded child can stray
 Beyond the Father's sight:

"That care and trial seem at last,
  Through memory's sunset air,
Like mountain-ranges overpast,
  In purple distance fair.

"That all the jarring notes of life
  Seem blending in a psalm;
And all the angles of its strife
  Slow rounding into calm.

"And so the shadows fall apart,
  And so the west winds play;
And all the windows of my heart
  I open to the day."

J. G. WHITTIER.

CHAPTER IX.

NERVOUS SENSITIVENESS AND INHARMONIOUS INFLUENCES.

The State Described — Susceptibility to the Influence of Others — Characteristic of Insanity — Disease the Ultimation of a prior Mental Disorder — Illustration from Molière — Effect of Inharmonious Influences upon Sensitives — Inanimate Objects — All Dwellings are Haunted — Food affected by the Mental Effluvia — Dr. Sweetser — Effect of Drug Medication — Necessity of the proper Sanative Conditions — Good the Goal of Ill.

THERE is a numerous class of invalids whose nervous system is so delicately and abnormally sensitive, that they are unduly affected by the sphere or influence of those in whose presence they happen to be. The diseased condition of others is transferred to them, and sometimes with little or no mitigation. As if by an unseen contagion, the pains and physical disorders of those surrounding them are communicated sympathetically to them. Especially are they affected by the disturbed mental states of others, which are immediately transmitted to them, subjecting them to much suffering, and producing an unbalanced spiritual condition, which seems to lie beyond their power to control. This is not, as is uncharitably supposed, the effect of imagination merely, but one of the most real things in human life, as many a nervous invalid too well knows from his own bitter experience. While the presence and aural emanation of those whose sphere is congenial and harmonious with their own, quiets and tranquillizes their disturbed mind and over-sensitive nerves, mitigates their sufferings, allays their unhealthy excitability, and exerts an unseen but potential sanative influence, the society of others intensifies every pain, accelerates the progress of their disease, and increases their mental and spiritual inharmony. Such a state of nervous sensitiveness is a morbid condition, though all are affected, more or less, by the persons and objects around them, only some in a much higher degree than others. It will be found that this is an almost invariable characteristic of insanity, nearly all insane patients being found highly sensitive to the sphere of their social surroundings; and when that influence is discordant, their cure is extremely difficult, not to say impossible, until they are removed beyond its reach. This is one of the main grounds on which physicians, who make a specialty of treating mental and cerebral diseases, recommend their removal to asylums, where they are supposed to be beyond the reach of this cause of disturbance and obstacle to a cure. But in very many cases, it is to be feared, that this course, instead of an alleviation, is only an aggravation of it, by crowding together the most heterogeneous and discordant spiritual elements, which mutually act and react upon each other, and this deleterious inharmonious influence is not unfrequently such, that under it the unfortunate patient passes to an incurable stage of his mental malady. Instead of arresting, it accelerates the morbid spiritual and cerebral condition, until it becomes confirmed, or the brain undergoes a retrograde metamorphosis or softening of its tissue.

Every unbalanced mental condition, according to the etymological sense of the term, is an insanity, or mental unsoundness, though the word is usually applied only to those extreme cases where there is a loss of control of the mental manifestations. Few, if any, chronic invalids can be found who are not the subjects of some serious spiritual disturbance, which is the primal source of their bodily disease. The cause of that long series of organic changes that constitute pathology is always psychical rather than somatic. A large proportion of chronic disorders, especially those of a nervous type, are characterized by an over-sensitive state of the nervous system, caused by an antecedent morbid mental excitement, and impressibility, and a confirmed habit of *thinking* that they are sick. Molière, the celebrated French dramatist, expresses an important principle of mental hygiene and psychological medicine, when in one of his plays, the *Malade Imaginaire*, he represents one of his characters, who had been busily occupied with some congenial and recreating labor, in the midst of such agreeable scenes and social influences as had caused him lively and pleasant emotions, as saying, "I am so busy that I have no time to think of my disease." In this case, as the author of "Passional Hygiene and Natural Medicine" remarks on the passage, it no longer exists, since he has found diversion of his thoughts and equilibrium of mind. Will it be said that it did not exist before, when he did think of it? That is a mistake; a man is really sick in mind when he believes himself sick. This disorder of the imagination, as it is called, gradually but surely leads to somatic or corporeal disease and lesion of the organs, accelerated, as it too frequently is, by the dangerous and damaging assistance of a physician, with his deleterious drugs, who oftener than otherwise confirms the patient in his fears and fixed belief. How to make the invalid forget his disease and the mental unhappiness that underlies it, so as to cure him of the fixedness of the idea that he is sick and the tendency perpetually to concentrate the consciousness upon the deranged organism, which in many cases amounts to a mild form of monomania, is the important practical question in his treatment. As a matter of no small importance, in some cases even a *sine qua non*, he must be freed, so far as practicable, from all inharmonious and disturbing influences. It intensifies his painful sensations, renders all the nerves of sensibility supernaturally, or at least abnormally, acute; and hence the thoughts are constantly directed to the diseased organs, as spontaneously as the needle to the pole, and thus increasing the physiological disturbance. It throws a pall of darkness upon the solitary ray of hope that may linger to illuminate his despair, and the lamp of life burns down to a smoking wick. The psychopathic treatment is well adapted to this class of invalids. In their susceptible state, it operates with an efficiency that borders on the miraculous.

The influence of inanimate objects is by no means unimportant in the case of those of great nervous sensitiveness. All houses, as Longfellow has said in one of his poems, are haunted houses, — pervaded by the subtle sphere of their former inhabitants, both the living and the dead, who are unperceived except by their influence. The walls of our dwellings, the furniture they contain, the works of art that ornament them, and the beds on which we repose at night, are charged and permanently impregnated with the material effluvia and psychical emanations of our persons and presence. Our mental states, our joys and sorrows, our hopes and despair, our tranquillity and disquietude, our peace and inharmonies, our loves and hates, are indelibly impressed upon them; and to the psychometric sense, which many invalids possess, they become apparent, and are *felt*, if not perceived by the interior vision. This arcane principle of modern science must not be ignored. A young girl, under my direction for the cure of a depressing monomania, a seeming case of obsession of two years' standing, aggravated by hereditary tendencies, insisted with the most urgent entreaty upon being removed to another house, affirming that in the place where she was, her recovery was an impossibility. Though reduced by weakness to the verge of dissolution, occasioned by protracted fasting, which rendered her nervous system still more intensely sensitive to invisible and discordant semi-psychical influences, her request was finally granted, when her convalescence became more rapid and marked at once. A change of place, if no more than from one room to another, has frequently a sanative effect. Beside the psychometric influence of the familiar objects of an apartment or house upon a sensitive subject, they become connected in the mind with his pains and unhappiness, and by a law of association recall and perpetuate them. They become a part of ourselves.

A somewhat distinguished physician and author avers that the food we eat is pervaded by the aural emanations and affected by the mental condition of those who prepare it for our tables. To the invalid it certainly seems far different when prepared by the hand of sympathetic friendship and kindness, than when coming from those who are uncongenial and toward whom he feels an involuntary antipathy and spontaneous repugnance. In illustration of the effects of this influence, too often ignored, he relates a fact in his own experience. He was called to dine in a house in which the funeral of a member of the family had been celebrated the day before. The house was filled with an invisible atmosphere of gloom. On eating of some bread, prepared the day before, he was soon after seized with a sense of grief and almost insupportable sorrow, without any apparent cause. He only found relief when, by an inverted action of the stomach, the spiritually-poisoned mass was ejected from the system, and thus prevented from entering into the composition of the tissues. All these things are of small moment to persons in sound health and in the full vigor of animal life, who are no more disturbed by them than would be the calm repose and negative happiness of the ox. But to those of refined mental organization and sensitive nervous temperament, rendered doubly acute by disease, they lose their character of insignificant trifles and morbid fancies.

What I have said of the bad effects of inharmonious influences upon nervous sensitives will apply to the use of medicines. In the practice of medical psychology, I have made it a general rule to require the patient to suspend the use of all other remedies except those of a hygienic nature, knowing that it is sometimes more difficult to neutralize the effects of drugs than to cure the diseases for which they are administered. Those of a poisonous nature operate to cure disease by creating another morbid condition inconsistent with the first. Hence the word Allopathy, which is composed of two Greek terms signifying another disease, has been used to designate this system. This, at best, is only exchanging one evil for another, or rather it is casting out demons by Beelzebub, rather than by the finger of God.

Psychopathy, in common with all therapeutic systems, will sometimes fail to cure certain persons, from the non-existence of the essential conditions of its restorative influence. Its effects are counterbalanced by the influence of opposing forces. In the absence of the necessary conditions, even Jesus, the Christ, could not perform mighty works of healing. Under these circumstances, it is as unreasonable to demand or expect a cure, as to require one to build a house with no materials with which to construct it, and no foundation on which to place it. The patient may be, from certain opposing circumstances, either in his own mental condition, or his inharmonious surroundings, not receptive of any sanative influence. This applies equally well to every method of healing in use in the world. The failure to effect a cure by physicians of any school is not always owing to the inefficiency of the remedial agencies employed in the case, or their want of chemical adaptation to the disease, but from circumstances beyond their control. In all these cases the true physician can only commend the patient to the care of a loving Providence, feeling assured that disorder has its laws and limitations, and suffering, both of body and mind, its compensations and rewards as a restorative spiritual discipline, and means of developing the inner nature. The great end of life and goal of human progression is an intimate and conscious union with God through the whole extent of our faculties, and the limitless period of the soul's duration. For this the inmost centre of our being ever yearns and to it perpetually gravitates. The route to its attainment sometimes lies through great tribulation. But, as Cousin, the French metaphysician, has said, no road is absolutely bad that conducts us to God.

GOOD THE FINAL GOAL OF ILL.

"Oh, yet we trust that somehow good
  Will be the final goal of ill,
  To pangs of nature, sins of will,
Defects of doubt and taints of blood;

"That nothing walks with aimless feet;
　That not one life shall be destroyed,
　Or cast as rubbish to the void,
When God hath made the pile complete;

"That not a worm is cloven in vain;
　That not a moth with vain desire
　Is shrivelled in a fruitless fire,
Or but subserves another's gain.

"Behold, we know not anything;
　I can but trust that good shall fall
　At last — far off — at last, to all,
And every winter change to spring.

"So runs my dream: but what am I?
　An infant crying in the night:
　An infant crying for the light:
And with no language but a cry."

　　　　　　　　　　　　　TENNYSON.

CHAPTER X.

THE DUALITY OF THE MIND AND BODY, AND THE POSITIVE AND NEGATIVE DISTINCTION IN THE PSYCHIC AND MAGNETIC FORCES OF THE ORGANISM.

Polar Distribution of Vital Magnetism — The Body a Complex Magnet — Numerous Poles — The Right Hand Positive — The Left Negative — The Two Sides — The Front and Back — Head and Feet — Difference between the Positive and Negative Forces explained — When to use the Right Hand — Philosophy of it — When the Left Hand is to be used — The Effect of Both — How to use them together — Two Kinds of Inflammation — Their Difference — How to Treat them — Circumstances of Secondary Importance favorable to the Curative Influence of Magnetism — The Duality of the Mind and Body — The Nature of Disease.

THE psychic and magnetic forces of the human body are analogous to ferro-magnetism, or the artificial magnet, in having a polar distribution. The two principal poles are the right and left hands. The right hand is positive, the left is negative. Besides these there are numerous others. The right and left sides all the way through are in magnetic opposition, but in a state of health so equally balanced as to be in equilibrium. The right side is positive, the left side is negative, through their entire extent. The same may be said of the front and back sides. The anterior portion is positive, the posterior is negative. In the female organism the opposite of this is true. The head and feet are the poles of the two extremities of the body. Hence counter-irritants are applied to the feet in inflammation of the brain. And where there is inflammation on one side of the body, the face, or one hand, or leg, it is always better to apply the irritant and stimulant to the opposite side. This produces what is called a derivative effect. This hint may be of use in the psychopathic treatment of a patient.

The difference between a positive and negative magnetic and psychological force, it may be difficult to explain so clearly as to be easily apprehended. It is to be understood in the outset that a negative force is no less real than a positive one. It is not the negation of a force, but one of an opposite and different character. Both are equally real. Action always implies reaction, and these are equal. A positive force, as in electricity, is that which is active; a negative force is reactionary, but still equal to the former. If the positive force is an undulation or vibratory movement,—and such are light, heat, electricity, and magnetism,—the negative would be expressed by an undulatory wave moving in the opposite direction, the waves being situated between the others. The magnetism of the right hand, or the positive pole of the animal magnet, is repellant and cooling; that of the left is attractive and warming. To the interior perception, the odyllic emanation of the right hand, like that of the north pole of the artificial magnet, is of a pale blue color, and produces a cooling sensation, like that of a gentle breeze, upon one sufficiently impressible to feel it. The emanation from the left hand, and the south pole of the magnet, is red, or white tinged with red, and produces a sensation of warmth. So of those two colors, the one is positive, the other odyllically negative. The right hand acts from without inward; the left hand from within outward. The one sends the force inward; the other attracts it from above downward, and from the interior to the surface. Where there is an inflammation or accumulation of positive psychic and magnetic life, it is to be dispersed by the positive or north pole of the human battery, — the right hand. The philosophy of this is plain. It is one of the most familiar phenomena of magnetism and electricity, that between positive and positive there is repulsion. Place the north poles of two magnets in contact, and they are immediately pushed apart. If the forebrain, which is positive, is hot and congested, place the right hand upon it, which is also positive, and it repels its accumulated magnetic force, and disperses the inflammation. It greatly assists in doing this, if the left hand be placed upon the back of the head, which will attract the magnetism of the forebrain and the right hand to it, for between negative and positive there is attraction. If there be coldness, or a lack of vitality, in any part, place the left hand over it, and the right hand on the opposite side or pole, and soon the distribution of the vital heat, or living organic force, will be equalized. It is always well to place the two hands on the opposite sides. If one is laid upon the epigastrium, or pit of the stomach, the other should be held upon the spine back of it. If one hand is placed on the right side of the brain, the other must be placed upon the left side. The psychic force will then pass from one hand to the other, and equalize the circulation of the imponderable and mysterious principle of life. Sometimes, as Deleutze remarks, the hands will feel as if they touched. This always indicates an efficient and favorable action of the subtle influence. Some persons also have a perception of the current as it flows from hand to hand. But this is not common.

I have said that inflammations are to be dispersed with the right hand. But there are both positive and negative inflammations and congestions. The one is an accumulation of negative, and the other of positive vital force. The pain of a positive inflammation is an ache; that of a negative more of a smarting sensation, and may be described sometimes as half way between an ache and a smart. Bear in mind that between negative and negative there is repulsion. You can disperse it then with the left hand, while you place the other upon the opposite side or pole. Or you can infuse into it the positive psychic force, using the right hand as a conductor.

It was found, by Reichenbach, that the rays of the sun falling upon his sensitives caused a sensation of coolness, while those of the moon and the planets, which shine by reflected light, were odyllically warm. A hot stove caused to the very sensitive a sensation of coldness, amounting almost to a frost, until they came so near it as to be affected by its radiated heat. This accounts for the depressing influence upon the vital force of an atmosphere heated by an iron stove. And I am convinced that the therapeutic results of this system of medical psychology can be best realized in a room which, though not dark, is but imperfectly lighted. It should also be only moderately heated, and, if possible, with an open grate, or fireplace, which is best of all, or with a soapstone stove. An apartment on the north side of the house is to be preferred. These may be deemed things of minor consequence, and certainly they are not to be classed among the "weightier matters of the law," yet they have their importance. One of the most successful healers, by this method of treatment, of whom I have ever read, Herr Richter, of Silesia, wore a loose scarlet robe, with which he sometimes struck the patient, commanding disease to depart. There may be philosophy in this, as red is a color magnetically and odyllically positive. There is often an unrecognized power and sanative value in little things, which might seem matters of indifference. We do well to learn what these things are, and avail ourselves of them.

The dual nature of man is an interesting subject of study, and has not received the attention its importance demands. There are two distinct departments of the mind, the intellectual and affectional. Each of these mental halves is a distinct, though not absolutely separate mind by itself. The difference in them is, that in the one the intellectual predominates, in the other the affectional and emotional. It is a fact of consciousness that there may be two synchronous trains of thought and feeling, which may be in harmony, or, as they often are, in conflict. The one is the normal, the other an abnormal and disturbed mental state. A loss of the due balance between the two departments of the mental structure lies at the root of most forms of mental disease and inharmony. When the two exist in equal degree, and act in perfect concert, just as both eyes see at once and alike the same object, it constitutes a condition of mental soundness, health and harmony. Corresponding to this peculiar mental organization, we have a bodily structure composed of two distinct parts. The whole human organism is, in the beginning, made up of two absolutely distinct halves, which ultimately grow together and unite. The brain, the organ of the mind, though not properly double, is dual in its structure and arrangement, as much so as the two eyes and the two ears and all the organs of sense. What is called the two *hemispheres* of the brain, separated from each other by a membrane dipping down between them (the *falx*), is a misnomer, as the two together constitute little more than half a sphere, and each by itself only about the fourth of a sphere. But there is reason to believe, and, in fact, has been demonstrated, that these twin halves are each a distinct and perfect whole as an organ of thought and feeling, and a separate and distinct process of thinking and reasoning may be carried on in each simultaneously and successively.* The desires and volitions of the one may be opposed to those of the other. This experience led the Persian monarch, Cyrus, according to Xenophon, to conclude that he had two souls. This inward conflict, this interior schism, is vividly described by Paul, in the seventh chapter of the epistle to the Romans. The perfect union of the divine love and divine wisdom in God makes him at the same time the Infinite Father and Mother, under which latter designation the world is just beginning to apprehend him. So "in the beginning, God made man male and female." Every human being has in himself the peculiarly masculine and feminine principles, the intellectual and affectional, the positive and negative, and these find their appropriate organ of external manifestation in the right and left sides of the brain and body. When these are perfectly combined and act in unison, we have the *mens sana in corpore sano*, the sound mind in a sound body; in other words, health and harmony. The excessive predominance of the positive over the negative, or of the negative over the positive,

* This subject has been thoroughly discussed, and illustrated by facts, in the able work of Dr. Wigan, entitled, "A New View of Insanity; or, the Duality of the Mind." The great objection to the work is found in its extreme materialistic views of human nature, an objection equally applicable to Maudsley, Winslow, and many others.

or the entire loss or suppression of one or the other, constitutes the state of inharmony we call mental and bodily disease;. a word made up of *dis*, without, and *ease*, and in its primary sense signifying uneasiness, disquietude, restlessness, and unhappiness. This loss of balance, which constitutes disease, we witness in an exaggerated degree in what is called *hemiplegia*. This is the typical representation of all disease, only existing in a marked and heightened form. To discover the cause of the lost balance and restore the harmony is the function of the psychopathic physician. Above all remedial agencies in nature, nothing is so well adapted to this result as an intelligent application of the principles of medical psychology. The subject of the duality of the mind and body deserves a more extended discussion than I can devote to it here. I can only hope that these hints and glimpses of thought may provoke in some mind a more extended investigation, which will certainly be repaid with a fruitful harvest of the best results.

All diseases may be reduced to two classes, the positive and negative. In the mental state, underlying the one class, the intellectual is in excess; in the other class the affectional. In the corresponding bodily condition we have, in the one case, an increased sensibility and heightened temperature; in the other, a cold, weakened, and devitalized state of the organism. Where there is an excess of positive magnetism in the patient, and this constitutes the morbid condition, it may be neutralized by the negative magnetism of some other person, for opposite magnetic forces neutralize each other, just as certainly as do acids and alkalies in chemical combinations.* If the disease be characterized by the predomi-

---

* I use the word magnetism as expressive of an analogy rather than an identity with the vital principle. The phrase, *psychic*

nance of the negative force, impart to the patient, from the stores of your own surplus, positive magnetic life, and this will benefit him just as surely as a too acid state of a substance may be neutralized by the mixture of an alkali with it. In this established principle, that a positive and negative magnetic force neutralize each other, is found the subtle chemical action that constitutes the *modus operandi* in many cases of sudden cures by the psychopathic treatment. Where the magnetism of the physician is perfectly adapted to the diseased condition of the patient, he may be as certain of affording relief, and ultimately of effecting a cure, as he can be that a heated substance will impart warmth to a cold one; that a darkened mansion may be made light and joyous by the admission of the sun's rays, or an acid neutralized by an alkali. Where the patient and physician are in opposite magnetic states, the cure will certainly follow the intelligent application of the treatment, if the disease has not passed into the incurable stage, and where this is manifestly the case, it will afford relief.

If the highest results in the psychopathic treatment are realized only where there is the widest difference in the magnetic condition of the patient and operator, it might seem that one person could not be adapted to only a certain class of cases, and not to each case that might come before him. This, to some extent, is true. One individual will produce a certain effect, or physiological change, as, for instance, perspiration, much more readily than another. Some will affect particular organs more readily than others, as the lungs, the liver, the stomach,

force, derived from a Greek word, signifying the mind or soul, and recently introduced by science to explain certain mysterious phenomena, is to be preferred. Of this the hands are the best conductors.

or the kidneys. Some are better adapted, as perhaps in my own case, to mental and nervous diseases. While all this is true, yet we can become positive or negative towards a patient at will. There are cases where we must assume a state of negative passivity towards the invalid, and others towards whom we must become intensely and actively positive. These magnetic transformations and metamorphoses can be easily effected, and they naturally and spontaneously follow the corresponding change in our mental attitude towards the patient. The only difficulty is to know when to become positive, and when negative, in order to adapt our magnetism to the demands of the particular case. But this we shall soon learn by practice and experience.

CHAPTER XI.

THE BRAIN AND PSYCHIC AND NERVE CENTRES.

Nerve Centres — Their Number and Location — Relation of the Brain to the general System — The Nerve Substance the Primary Seat of Disease — The Brain the Fountain of Psychic Life — Its Susceptibility to Magnetism — Directions in Treating it — Excess to be Avoided — The Imparted Magnetism not to be left there — How to Distribute it where it is needed — Connection of the Bodily Organs with certain Parts of the Cerebrum — The State of these Parts an Index to that of the Organs — The Seat of Muscular Force — An Illustrative Case — The Liver and the Brain — Kidneys — The Bowels — Duodenum — The Diaphragm — How to Increase the Respiratory Force — The Cure of Asthma — Catarrh — How the Magnetism of the Brain affects the whole Body — Functions of the Cerebellum.

THERE are certain parts of the body which may be properly denominated magnetic centres. The psychopathic treatment of those points affects a large number of organs, perhaps all the organs within the cavity of the trunk which are situated above and below them. These centres and reservoirs for the distribution of the psychic and nervous life are the brain, the spine, the epigastrium, the abdominal and hypochondriac regions.

The brain is the fountain of all nerve force, and to restore this organ to a harmonious and healthy action, goes far towards a restoration of the whole system to a sound physiological condition, for every part of the organic structure is connected with the brain, and communicates with it, by means of the spine and the nerves.

These are continuations of the brain into the body. If we purify this fountain of life from disease, the stream soon runs clear. It is a well-established fact of pathology, that disease has its primary seat in some abnormal state of the nervous system. All diseases, though they may originate in some prior disturbed mental and spiritual states, first affect the nerves. All morbid conditions are, so far as the body is concerned, originally and primarily nervous diseases. The brain and nerves are first affected, before the various bodily organs are deranged in their functional movements. This would seem unerringly to indicate that the brain should receive marked attention in the cure of disease by the psychopathic method, and even by any system of medication. We must begin the cure where the disease commences. It is a common observation, that if the head feel well, we feel well everywhere. It is equally true that if the brain is in an abnormal state, the system is generally deranged. It is a fortunate circumstance that the cerebral tissue seems to be more susceptible to the magnetic and psychic influence than any other part of the organism. The hands, properly applied to the brain, will soon restore the lost harmony in the circulation and distribution of the forces that here have their origin. When this reservoir of life and health is repaired, a healthy vital current will be conveyed by the nerves to every other organ and tissue. Place the hands, one on the forebrain and the other upon the occiput or back of the head, and gently press on those parts. Apply them also to the sides in the same manner. Pass the hand from the forehead around the side over the temples, and also over the brain, from the front to the back brain, along the mesial line, or the line dividing the two hemispheres. Apply vigorous friction with the left hand to the back brain and neck. Then place the hands upon the shoulders for a moment, and apply friction and pressure to the arms, and the spine, and sometimes, if the case requires it, also to the abdomen and lower extremities. This will serve to restore harmony to the brain, and cause a diffusion of its nerve force to all the organs of the body, — an important point to be gained, and one that cannot be so well effected by the administration of medicines. There are few chronic invalids who would not feel better by such a treatment. In fact, it will suffice to cure a large fraction of chronic ailments that come under the care of a physician. Who has not felt invigorated and refreshed after the head has been rubbed and champooed by the barber? And the old lady came to her bishop and requested him to repeat the rite of confirmation, because the imposition of his hands was good for her rheumatism.

Owing to the extreme susceptibility of the brain to the psychic influence, a prolonged and excessive treatment of it must be avoided. An error here is not uncommon. From one to five minutes will suffice. If you have much magnetic force, a single minute will often be enough.

The magnetism imparted to the brain should not, as a general rule, be left here, except in cases where there is a lack of magnetic life in it, and it is cold and sluggish, but it should be attracted downward to the organs of the body, by passing the hand down the spine, and sometimes by rubbing and kneading the whole body, flexing and extending the limbs, and bending the joints. This is not always necessary, and is laborious and exhausting. By passing the hand downward, it will serve to restore the nervous connection between the brain and the various organs and parts of the body.

Some defect in this communication is often the cause of disease. The nerve force, instead of being dispersed to every part of the body, accumulates in the brain, and mental disturbance and inharmony, and a weakness in the functional activity of the various organs, are the result.

It is now well established in physiology, that each of the principal organs of the body, as the heart, the lungs, the liver, the stomach, the intestinal canal, and the kidneys, receives its nerve force and stimulus from a certain part of the brain, which is assigned to its special function. This is why a judicious treatment of the brain favorably affects every organ in the body. Disease of the liver, or obstinate constipation, or dyspepsia, or a derangement of the kidneys and renal functions, is indicated by the condition of certain parts of the cerebrum. I have never found much difficulty in gaining a correct diagnosis of the diseased condition of a patient from an examination of the state of the brain.

There is a part of the brain, situated midway between firmness and self-esteem, in which all voluntary muscular force and physical strength originates. In cases of general organic weakness, and the different forms of female diseases arising from debility, this place will be found sensitive to pressure, and will be inflamed and congested. Sometimes the patient cannot bear the pressure of the head against the back of a chair. Some years ago a lady, of about thirty years of age, was brought to me, who had not walked ten rods at one time for nine years. She was brought into the house in the arms of another and laid upon the bed. The next morning, on examining her case, no serious organic disease could be detected, and no great derangement or displacement of the uterine organs, but only a general weakness everywhere.

The part of the brain before mentioned was tender and congested. I informed her where the trouble was situated, and that I could cover it with the palm of my hand. I proceeded to treat her on the supposition that this part of the cerebrum was alone at fault, cooled its inflammation by the magnetism of the hand wet in water, and dispersed its accumulated nerve-force to the general organism which needed it. The whole system seemed to be restored to a healthy tone at once. She could walk for miles without fatigue, and has continued well to the present date. Other facts equally interesting might be given.

The liver receives its peculiar cerebral or nerve stimulus, from a part of the brain situated between combativeness and cautiousness; the kidneys from a point on each side of causality; the bowels from the part of the brain between hope and veneration. In some forms of dyspepsia the brain is affected between benevolence and veneration. Inflammation of the duodenum is indicated by a spot tender to pressure situated half way between the angle of the eye and the ear. The sore eyes that accompany it are immediately relieved by cooling this part of the brain.

There is no physiological function of more consequence than the respiration. A good respiration is of equal importance with a good digestion. The more one breathes, the stronger he is. The breathing force is supplied by the diaphragm, the lungs being wholly passive in the act. There is a part of the brain just above the nose, and above and between the eyes, that seems to be assigned to the function of respiration. It is in the region of the frontal sinus. By removing the tightness and congestion here, a patient will spontaneously draw a deep breath. Asthma is occasioned by a want of nervous force in the diaphragm, and a consequent loss of its contractility. Catarrh is its incipient stage, and originates in the same cause. Both are exceedingly difficult to cure by medicine. Medical science has no reliable and certain remedy for either. But the magnetism of the hand applied to the region of the brain above described, so as to relieve its congestion, and determine its accumulated nerve-force to the diaphragm, will relieve and cure both complaints. While medicine can only afford a temporary alleviation of the symptoms, this goes to the root of the malady, and effects a fundamental change. These discoveries were made by the interior vision, usually called clairvoyance, and have been confirmed by experiment. After many years of patient investigation, I am convinced of their correctness and practical value in the treatment of disease by psychic remedies.

In another way an intelligent treatment of the brain may be made to affect favorably the action of all the vital organs. The cerebrum, or the front and large part of the brain, is the organ of our voluntary life. The involuntary functions of the different portions of the system are influenced by the cerebellum, or little brain, situated in the back of the head, and below the other. Now it usually happens that the large brain has too great a share of the nerve-force, or what has been improperly called the nerve-aura, and consequently robs the cerebellum of its proper proportion, and thus weakens the involuntary physiological processes. By placing the right or positive hand upon the forebrain, it repels its superabundant psychic life backward, while the left hand, at the same time placed upon the cerebellum, attracts it to that part of the brain. There is added to it also the magnetic force of the operator. Thus all the involuntary vital processes, as the action of the heart and lungs, the necessary functions of digestion, secretion, excretion, assimilation and absorption, are stimulated to a more vigorous activity. By the new life thus imparted to the cerebellum, and of which it had been robbed by the over-action of the cerebrum, a healthy impulse is given to all these vital movements. This single form of treatment will be found extremely useful and recuperative in nearly all forms of chronic ailments, for they often consist in a debilitated action of the involuntary physiological functions, owing to a weakened condition of the cerebellum. By restoring the lost equilibrium in the nervous force of these two departments of the cerebral organism, a cure is effected.

The cerebellum, besides its being the organ of the amative sexual instinct, has other important functions, and when stimulated by the subtle magnetic and psychic force, important effects cannot fail to be produced. The discoveries of Mr. Atkinson, as recorded in the "Zoist" (Vol. 1, p. 249), have been confirmed by my own experiments and investigations. According to him, that portion of the cerebellum nearest the ear gives *the disposition to muscular action;* next to which, and about half way between the ear and the occiput on the top of the cerebellum, is *muscular sense;* beneath this is *muscular power*, giving force and strength. In the centre are what may be termed the physico-functional powers, a group of organs giving the sense of physical pleasure and pain, the sense of temperature, amativeness, etc. It is intuitively certain, and confirmed by observation and consciousness, that the tendency to muscular action, the sense of bodily pain and pleasure, and also of temperature, are affected by the state of the amative propensity, and the portion of the little brain consecrated to its function. When a subject is in the impressible condition, by applying the finger to that part of the cerebellum which gives us the sense of temperature, and thus augmenting its action, there is first experienced a pleasant glow of heat over the surface of the body, and this, if continued, is followed soon by a gentle perspiration. The cerebellum is a finely adjusted battery and reservoir of magnetic life and vital force. Its full development and healthy state are indicative, not only of the strength of the sexual love, as in the system of Gall, but what is of equal importance of the *quantum* of vital and muscular force in the organism. Its judicious psychopathic treatment must be followed by important therapeutic results. The influence is not local, or limited to the point of contact, but widely diffused through the entire physiological domain.

CHAPTER XII.

EFFECT OF THE PSYCHOPATHIC TREATMENT OF THE SPINE AND SPINAL NERVES.

The Spinal Column a Magnetic Centre — Its Relation to the Functions of Organic Life — The Ganglia and their Use — The Divisions of the Spine — Their distinct Functions — The Spinal Nerves — A rational Pathology of Nervous Diseases — Loss of Balance between the Motory and Sensory Nerves — The Cure of Nervous Invalidism Simple and Easy — The Method described — Adaptation of the Spinal Nerves to the Magnetic Treatment — How it Affects all the Organs in the Cavity of the Trunk — How to Relieve Spinal Irritation and Inflammation — Philosophy of it — The Small of the Back.

ANOTHER important nerve-centre, whence a vital influence may be distributed to a large number of organs, is the spinal column, commencing in the medulla oblongata and extending through the length of the trunk of the body. It is now an universally acknowledged and recognized truth of physiology, that the spine sustains an important relation to, and connection with, the involuntary vital processes, of equal importance with that of the brain itself, of which it is the continuation. Its numerous ganglia, or knots, seem to be each a little brain, and an independent centre and reservoir for the distribution of the nervous and psychic forces. These closely resemble the circular swellings on the stalk of wheat and most of the grasses. They are laid in a regular series down each side of the spine, and are connected by the great sympathetic nerve. There are other ganglia in the cavities of the chest and abdomen. It is quite possible and not beyond the range of actual fact, that the vital functions might be performed by the spinal nerves alone, for a longer or shorter period, when the brain was entirely quiescent, or even removed. But only the phenomena of the involuntary, or what has been called the vegetative life would be exhibited under those circumstances. The vital machinery would continue in motion, but without any consciousness of its movement by the individual.

Different columns of nervous matter combine to form the spinal marrow. It may be separated laterally into two general divisions. Each of these consists of three cords, one for motion, one for sensation, and one for the act of respiration. So that the spinal marrow consists, in all, of six rods bound together. The anterior column of each lateral division is for motion, the posterior for sensation, and the middle portion for respiration. The former two extend into the brain and are lost in it. The latter terminates in the medulla oblongata, which crowns the compound column, as the function of respiration can be carried on independent of the reason and will. Thirty-one pairs of nerves proceed from the spine along its entire extent. These proceed from the spine in two distinct roots, which unite to form the trunk of the nerve. The front root is motory or employed in motion; the posterior root is sensory. *A loss of balance between these two classes of nerves is sometimes a source of disease.* This is perhaps uniformly the case in what are called nervous complaints. The sensations of the patient become morbidly acute, while there is a corresponding loss of the power of motion and a *disinclination* to it. They suffer much, not from the absolute amount of pain, but from their extreme sensitiveness to it. A judicious psychopathic treatment is adequate to restore the lost harmony, by restoring to the nerves of motion their share of the cerebral force, and lessening that of the sensory nerves. In such patients, the respiration is always feeble and imperfect, and general weakness is the result. The psychic force imparted by the physician will stimulate the respiratory cord of the spinal column. This will be better than any tonic or stimulant known to medical science. The skilful practitioner can direct his psychological force to either class of nerves. It obeys his will, and goes where he commands it. In most nervous invalids the nerve aura or force, generated in the brain and spine, is appropriated by the sensory nerves, and this monopoly leaves the motory nerves in an enfeebled condition proportioned to the degree of the inharmony. These latter nerves, by this deficient supply of their appropriate stimulus, and from a want of use, become too soft, and exhibit too great a degree of transparency, while the matter of a nerve in health and the due exercise of its influence is of an opaque white hue, and half way between a fluid and solid. If I have given the correct pathology of what are called nervous diseases, which constitute in their treatment a large proportion of the practice of the physician, the method of cure would seem to be a simple one. The lost harmony between the two classes of nerves must be restored. The nerves of motion must be stimulated to life and activity to balance and to diminish the too great action of the nerves of sensation. The great question is, How can this best be done? Fortunately nature has so arranged the nerves of motion as if purposely to adapt them to be acted upon by the magnetism of the hand. The motory nerves, before they are distributed to the muscular tissue of the various organs and parts of the body, are formed into a sort of network by an interchange of branches. They cross each other and unite with each other, into an intricate mass or web, called a plexus. The most important of these are the brachial and lumbar plexus, the one situated between the shoulders, and the other in the loins or small of the back. The plexus between the shoulders is formed by the interlocking and interlacing of six pairs of motory nerves. These after their union are distributed to the arms, the diaphragm, the intercostal muscles (or those between the ribs concerned in respiration), the heart and the lungs. The connection of these nerves constitutes a sympathetic communication between these parts and organs. The subtle psychic magnetism of the hand applied between the shoulders improves the tone and adds to the muscular vigor and strength of them all. If you affect one, you affect the whole. The sympathy existing between them may be seen in the movement of the arms and the motion of the diaphragm and lungs. To swing your arms necessitates an accelerated and increased action of the lungs and diaphragm in breathing. To strengthen the arms improves the tone and vigor of all the muscles concerned in respiration.

So the motory nerves of the lower extremities and those of the kidneys, the reproductive organs, and the large intestine, are all united into a sympathetic plexus in the small of the back. In nervous diseases, which are so common, there is a lack of healthy tone in the nerves of motion of these parts, and an over-sensitiveness in the nerves of feeling. This will be found to be a uniform characteristic in the pathology of nervous invalidism. To restore the harmony is to effect a cure. This can be sooner done by the judicious and persevering use of the psychopathic treatment than by any other remedial agency. It is better than all narcotics and nervines that were ever prescribed.

From what has been said of the relation of the spinal nerves to the involuntary vital processes and movements, it must be evident that the magnetism of the hand, applied to the spine, will affect all the internal organs. By the friction of the hand along the spinal column, an invigorating, life-giving influence is imparted to all the organs within the cavity of the trunk. The hand of kindness, of purity, and of sympathy, applied here, by friction combined with gentle pressure, is a singularly efficient remedy for the morbid condition of the internal organs. It is a medicine that is always pleasant to take.

The diseased condition of the truncal organs is often indicated by tenderness in the corresponding parts of the spine. The spine at certain points will be found inflamed and congested. The psychopathic treatment will almost always be sufficient to relieve and remove the morbid state of the parts. To pour water, of the temperature of about one hundred degrees, along the whole length of the spine, commencing in the neck, and delaying at the inflamed points, will relieve the congestion. It may be poured in a small stream from the nose of a pitcher. The philosophy of its action is plain. In all congestions there is a tightening up of the tissue. Now it is known that heat expands and relaxes all substances in nature, with only one known exception, — the thawing of ice. We see a thousand illustrations of this law. The warm water applied to the congested and tightened fibres and tissue of the inflamed parts expands and relaxes them, and thus restores the obstructed circulation. Still further, we know from our frequent experience, that the reaction which follows holding the hands or feet in warm water is cooling. They soon feel cooler than before their immersion in it. So it is in the application of warm water to the spine. The reaction which follows plunging the feet in cold water increases vital action and warms them. It will be found, in harmony with this philosophy, that warm water is more effectual in allaying inflammations than cold water. Inflamed eyes are greatly aggravated by the application of cold water; but are relieved and soothed by tepid water. To understand nature's laws is to be invested with power to cure disease. For there can be no miraculous cure of the sick. No restoration can be effected by men or angels, in contravention of the uniform and undeviating laws of our being.

The small of the back or loins is the weak or strong point in every person. This part of the spine is the symbol of strength. It is an important centre of voluntary motion, and should always receive a due share of attention in the psychopathic treatment of disease. Nearly three hundred muscles are directly or indirectly connected with the motions of which the small of the back is the pivotal centre. Persons who are strong, and whose muscular system is vigorous and well-balanced, never complain of weakness here, while invalids will almost always be found to suffer from weakness and pain in this part of the body. The magnetism of the hand applied here is the most efficient remedy in nature, especially when accompanied by the kneading and upward pressure of the abdomen. A large proportion of chronic diseases are immedially relieved and ultimately cured by this simple treatment.

CHAPTER XIII.

THE APPLICATION OF THE PSYCHIC AND MAGNETIC FORCE TO THE EPIGASTRIUM, AND THE NATURE AND CURE OF NERVOUS DISEASES.

The Pit of the Stomach a Vital Centre — Effect of a Blow here — It is Life's Last Retreat and Citadel — Accumulation of Nerve-Force here the Characteristic of Nervous Debility — Pathological State described — Robbery of the other Organs — State of the Diaphragm — The Stomach — Liver — Spleen — The Heart — Cause of their enfeebled Action — How to Effect a Cure — Directions in the Application of Magnetism to the Epigastric Region — Their Rationale and Efficiency — Immediate and Remote Effects.

THE epigastrium, or, as it is usually called, the pit of the stomach, is one of the most important nerve centres in the whole organism, and must claim special attention in the administration of Medical Psychology as a remedial agency. In this region is situated the semilunar ganglion and solar plexus, one of the largest in the great sympathetic nerve, which has been properly called the nerve of organic life. The presence of this large ganglion and plexus of nerves, which lie just under the diaphragm, and behind the stomach, constitutes, if not an independent, yet a most important vital centre. This is the reason why a blow on the pit of the stomach sometimes destroys life. In the process of dying, the vital force lingers here after it has retreated from the rest of the body. It often remains warm long after the rest of the organism has become cold and motionless. It is also the focal point of spiritual influx, and is singularly sensitive to the action of the psychic force. These facts and phenomena clearly indicate the essential relation of this region to the functions of organic life. In a large proportion of chronic diseases, especially those attended with nervous debility and prostration, it will be found to be the weak point, and will demand particular attention. In these cases the nerve-life seems to be concentrated here, and it becomes the focal point of their existence. One nervous invalid declared that she lived only in the pit of the stomach. Both the nerves of motion and of sensibility are acutely alive. There is unusual nervous heat at this point, and great tenderness to the touch, the patient being here so sensitive as to be able to bear scarcely the weight of the finger, not because a slight pressure occasions absolute pain, but the parts shrink from the touch, like the leaves of the sensitive plant, and there is an unpleasant feeling as if the vital spark was being suffocated. In fact, only a slight blow would extinguish the flame of life. The nerves of motion act spontaneously, and occasion an incessant crawling of the muscular fibres, and a nervous tremor, which is aggravated by the least excitement. This accumulation of the nerve-force in the pit of the stomach robs the adjacent organs of their rightful share, and weakens their physiological movements. The diaphragm loses its contractility and convexity, so that the respiration is enfeebled and the breathing is short and unsatisfactory. The stomach is enfeebled in its action, its vermicular motion soon gives out from a lack of nervous force, and indigestion is the result. The action of the heart is weakened and quickened and, under excitement, the patient suffers from palpitation. The liver is inflamed and congested, and, from a lack of vital force, performs its appropriate functions imperfectly. There is usually, also, a pain in the left side, which occasions the patient great anxiety, as it is erroneously supposed to be a disease of the heart, but it is in fact only an inflammation and enlargement of the spleen, which arises from a diminished supply of its nerve-force.

This will be found to be an accurate diagnosis of a large share of chronic ailments, especially those of a nervous type. The nature of the trouble will unerringly indicate the method of cure. In these cases the condition of the diaphragm, and the shortness of the breath, the enfeebled action of the stomach and heart, the sluggish state of the liver and spleen, and their enlargement, are effects, and we must find and remove the cause. The pathological condition arises solely from the concentration and accumulation of the nerve-force in the epigastrium, and the consequent robbery of the adjacent organs of their proper share. The cure must necessarily consist in restoring the harmony in the distribution of the nerve life. Its accumulated stores must be dispersed from the pit of the stomach and its excess diminished to supply the lack of it in the other organs. This is clear and simple. It only remains to point out the best method of cure. Bear in mind, that the diseased condition I have described is not an isolated case, but in all its essential features is the pathological state of a large proportion of chronic invalids. There may be found slight modifications of it in some nervous patients, but the treatment that will answer for one will be equally applicable to all cases.

Commence by inducing the impressible state of the patient by the process previously described. Treat the brain and spine as before recommended. Then place the right hand on the pit of the stomach. It may be placed in actual contact, or, in extremely sensitive cases, it may be held only quite near the parts. There will usually be found in these cases an inflamed and tender point in the spine, and sometimes an outward curvature, just back of the stomach. Place the left hand on this part of the spinal column, with a gentle pressure forward, so as to throw the body into an erect attitude. While the right hand remains upon the pit of the stomach, after a while, remove the left hand to the region of the lumbar plexus or small of the back. After a few minutes, make dispersive passes with the right hand over the hypochondriac region or the parts of the abdomen on each side of the epigastrium. This will attract the accumulated magnetic life from the pit of the stomach to the organs each side of it. You have now afforded relief. But more remains to be done to effect a radical and lasting cure. Place the left hand on the right side, just under the right shoulder, and as far down as the ribs extend. Place the right hand on the left side of the patient just under the ribs, near the end of the stomach and spleen. Then press with the hands, so as to effect a movement of the organs situated between the hands. Then change the position of the hands, the left hand being placed upon the back of the patient on the left side, and the right hand more in front near the liver and right end of the stomach. Repeat this several times. This alternate pressure effects a movement of the diaphragm, the liver, the stomach and the spleen. It will be found a sovereign remedy for inactivity of those organs. It is an invariable law, that the motion of a part determines the nervous and vital forces to the part moved. The movement of the hand in the act of opening and shutting it calls the vital force to that extremity. So of the arm, the foot, or the leg. By the motion of the organs which have been weakened in their action by a want of nerve-force, occasioned by its accumulation in the epigastrium, the vital force is determined to them. It attracts the excessive supply of nerve-life in the pit of the stomach into their own nerves, and thus improves at once their tone and vigor. No single treatment is of greater value than this, or better adapted to a large class of chronic diseases. It is oftentimes astonishing, and seems, to those who do not understand the laws governing the case, to border on the miraculous, to witness the rapid improvement that uniformly follows this apparently simple treatment. A single treatment often effects a permanent cure. I could give instances of immediate restoration to health of cases deemed hopeless for years, by the intelligent application of this method of cure, that might be deemed incredible, except by those who personally knew the facts, — cases that have occurred not only in my own practice, but in that of many others. We are not always to judge of the therapeutic value of Medical Psychology from the immediate and visible effects of a single treatment, or the employment of it for a few days. Sometimes a patient receives an impulse in an upward course, which results in a complete restoration to health, when the immediate effects are not so obvious. Instantaneous and apparently miraculous cures are not always the greatest cures effected by the psychopathic treatment. Patients are often found where the forces of life and the tendency to dissolution are so evenly balanced as to be in equilibrium. A feather's weight would turn the scale either way. The tendency of the nerve-force to the epigastrium is one of the phenomena of the process of dying. This is the last citadel in which life takes refuge from the invader, the last fortress that surrenders. A single application of the psychic and magnetic force turns the scale, reinforces the vital powers, invigorates the reaction of nature against the disease, and inaugurates a change which results in a radical cure, yet the immediate and visible effects may not be very obvious. Such cures are as miraculous as any that were ever wrought, and although they may not give a physician fame and wide-spread celebrity, no one should be disheartened if he cannot perform a cure which shall seem nearer to a miracle than this. Nature, unaided, is often adequate to cure disease. The patient gets well from the reaction of the vital force against the diseased state, when the *vis medicatrix naturæ*, the healing power of nature, is not interfered with, and obstructed in its action, by poisonous drugs. When nature requires assistance, nothing seems better adapted to render that aid than this mode of treatment. In this numerous class of diseases, medicines seem to have but little sanative value. They often produce directly opposite effects from those desired and intended. The psychic and magnetic force, properly applied and directed, is not a mere temporary stimulus, but imparts the living principle itself, and adds to the vital stock of the patient. I deem the principles relating to the pathology and cure of nervous diseases, so briefly unfolded in this chapter and the preceding, of great value. They contain the undeveloped germ of a volume. They place the subject in a new light. They are confessedly the most difficult class of diseases to control under the ordinary systems of medication. The physician expects only to relieve the morbid symptoms by his prescriptions. But the psychopathic treatment is peculiarly adapted to them, and goes to the root of the malady.

CHAPTER XIV.

THE ABDOMINAL MUSCLES AND THE MECHANICAL DISPLACEMENT OF THE INTERNAL ORGANS.

Theory of Chronic Diseases — Nature's Mode of Cure — Cause of the Prolapsed State of the Organs — How the Psychopathic Treatment removes it — The Method of Treating the Abdominal and Pelvic Viscera — Philosophy of it — The Practice of Mesmer and D'Eslon — Female Diseases — Their Cure — Communication of Vital Force — Derivative Effects — Pathology of Epilepsy — Nature's Sovereign Remedy for it.

IT was a theory advocated with much zeal by Dr. Banning, several years ago, that nearly all chronic diseases originate in a mechanical displacement, or falling down, of the organs within the cavity of the trunk. He supposed that there was no defect in the vital force; but, in chronic disease, the machinery was out of place, and consequently went wrong. It was a favorite maxim with him, "that it is not the *steam*, but the disturbed or broken engine that is at fault." I have no doubt of the substantial correctness of this theory, at least so far as it relates to the effect of the displacement of the organs, but should differ widely from him in regard to the proper remedy. Instead of applying artificial support, in the use of the various forms of abdominal supporters, which at best afford only a temporary relief, with an aggravation of the trouble in the end, it would be nature's method, and the remedy dictated by common sense, to go to work to strengthen and improve the tone of the muscular bands, composing the walls of the abdomen, and which are the natural supports of the organs. If these muscles lose their healthy tone, and become relaxed, exhibiting a soft and flabby state, all the organs are prolapsed by their own gravity. The heart and lungs, the diaphragm, the stomach, the liver, the spleen, and the bowels, by their gravitating tendency downward, press upon the pelvic viscera, and push these down also. It is plain to every one that the organs thus misplaced cannot properly perform the physiological functions assigned them in the animal economy. It is not uncommon to find patients where there is little or no organic disease, but a general lack of physical and muscular force, owing to a loss of harmony between the motory and sensory nerves. The abdominal muscles are relaxed, and lose their healthy contractility, and all the truncal organs are projected downward in a mass, crowding one upon the other, and thus interfering with their normal action. This is the pathological state of three-fourths of chronic invalids, and of females there is a still larger fraction.

This mechanical displacement of the organs is caused, immediately, by the weakness of the abdominal muscles, and this may be occasioned by a general loss of vital tone, and of the muscular tissue in particular. So far as this is the case, the psychopathic treatment will be found a sovereign remedy. For it is an admitted truth that one person can impart vital force to another who lacks it. This is just as certain as that one body can receive heat from another possessing more of it and in contact with it. The vital magnetism of a good practitioner imparts to the organism of the patient a life-giving principle, call it by what name you please. To me, this has the force of a self-evident truth. The whole subject has been fully illustrated and proved in the previous work of the author, the "Mental Cure," and it is unnecessary to dwell upon it here. The psychopathic treatment, by improving the general vital tone of the patient, and augmenting everywhere the vital force, improves the state of the abdominal muscles. But the magnetism of the hands applied here is a specific for their relaxed and debilitated condition. It imparts a healthy tone to them at once, and restores their diminished contractility. It affords to the parts a natural and healthy stimulus.

Let the patient sit in an erect attitude, with the pit of the stomach thrown forward. Place one hand on the spine, back of the stomach, or on the small of the back, and request the patient to slowly raise the arms, as high as he can reach. This elevates the ribs, and the diaphragm which is attached to them, and draws the muscular bands of the abdomen tense. Press the bowels up with the other hand. The arms are to be held in this elevated position only a moment, and then gently lowered. This alternate raising and lowering of the arms may be repeated several times. Friction may be applied to the abdomen, the hand always following the course of the large intestine or colon. That is, the movement must commence near the right groin, proceed upward to the top of the bowels, then across and downward. The bowels may be kneaded by pressing with the fingers on one side, and then with the ball of the hand on the opposite side, commencing with the lower part of the abdomen and proceeding upward to the stomach. This agitates the contents of the stomach and intestinal canal, and assists their natural functions, and is the best substitute for their peristaltic or vermicular movement, of which there is generally a lack. It improves the tone of the abdominal muscles, for it is a law, as we have already seen, that the movement of a part determines the vital force to the part moved. The kneading of any of the muscles is one of the best ways of increasing both their size and vigor. It stimulates the nutritive vessels of the parts, and increases their growth. The physician's hand also imparts a subtle vital magnetism and psychic force to the muscular tissue. While the treatment of the epigastrium or pit of the stomach should always be of a gentle and tranquillizing character, here it may be more vigorous and stimulating, but never too violent. This treatment, followed up, is a sure remedy for dyspepsia, inaction of the liver and kidneys, for obstinate constipation, a fruitful source of disease, and for the evils arising from the misplacement of the internal organs. It is the effectual mode of treating all forms of female diseases and prolapsus of the pelvic vicsera, as it seems to have a special adaptation to this part of the body. It was a part of the method of magnetizing employed by Mesmer and D'Eslon, to employ repeated pressure upon the hypochondriac and abdominal regions. This was sometimes continued for hours. In my opinion it had more to do in effecting the cures wrought by them than any other feature of the process which they used. It produces a powerful derivative effect, by determining the nerve-force from the brain, where it is usually in excess, downward to the organs that need it. By a proper treatment here, the muscles of the abdomen are restored to a healthy tone, the internal machinery is brought into proper position, and the organs resume a healthy functional activity. By simply placing the hands, one on the spine and the other over the organs within the abdominal or pelvic cavities, the subtle magnetic influence, differing in this respect from the electric, which is confined to the surface, penetrates the tissue, passes from one hand to the other, or is absorbed as a healthy vital force and stimulus by the several organs. Rapid and often astonishing improvement follows the application of this potent therapeutic agent to this part of the organism.

There is one disease impossible to cure by any medicine known to exist, for which it seems to be a specific. I refer to epilepsy. This terrible disease seems to commence in the state of the bowels. The symptoms of an attack are a peculiar sensation, first in the intestinal tube, and then in the stomach. This is a suspension of the vermicular movement peculiar to those organs, and then an inversion of the peristaltic motion. The nerve-force moves in the wrong direction, slowly moving upward through the intestinal canal to the stomach, and thence to the top of the brain. This inverted action of the nerves has been denominated the *aura epileptica*, and is accompanied by a strange morbid sensation commencing in some part of the intestinal canal, and gradually ascending to the cerebrum. This progress the patient can trace in his own feelings. The rush of the blood to that part of the brain, occasioned by the accumulation there of the nerve-force, presses upon the brain, and the patient loses all consciousness and muscular power and suddenly falls as if shot. The trouble arising from a suspension of the natural peristaltic movement of the parts, and the upward movement of the nerve-force, the cure must consist in finding a substitute for the one and thus preventing the other. A quick pressure of the fingers on one side of the abdomen, followed by a pressure of the hand upon the opposite side, and the same alternate pressure applied also to the right and left end of the stomach, is the best substitute nature has provided for their vermicular movement. This arrests at once the upward tendency of the nerve-force, and wards off the fit. The patient can do this himself on feeling the symptoms of an attack, or some member of the family may perform this office. I have never known a case where it would not prevent an attack, and if followed up effect a lasting cure. It is nature's remedy, and, consequently, the most efficient remedial agency. Where all medicines are confessedly powerless to afford relief this will succeed, if the disease has not passed to the incurable stage. Where it has reached its ultimate termination, in what Dr. Winslow denominates a "retrograde metamorphosis" of the cerebral tissue, or in plainer language, an actual softening of the brain, there is no cure for it, except the universal panacea, death. Previous to this stage I have never known it to fail. I have no disposition to sell the secret, but freely impart it to the world. Whoever reads this is invited to try it the first opportunity which occurs. If it succeeds, you have done a good work. If it fails, it will only do what all other remedies before it have done.

CHAPTER XV.

CONDUCTORS AND THEIR USE IN MEDICAL PSYCHOLOGY.

The Nerves are Conducting Wires — Identity of Magnetism and the Nervous Force — The Fluid Theory Exploded — How to affect an Organ through its Nerve — Illustrated by Sciatic Rheumatism — Why the Foot goes to Sleep — Effect of a Blow upon the Ulnar Nerve — Importance of Understanding the Anatomy of the Nervous System — Illustrations — The Trifacial Nerve — How to Cure Neuralgia of the Face and Teeth — The Optic Nerve — Amaurosis — Instant Relief for Inflamed Eyes — Treatment of Deafness — Ear-ache — The Pneumogastric Nerve — Its General Distribution — Its Function — How to Affect any Part or Organ through it — Vital Magnetism Controlled by the Will — Goes where it is Sent — Also spontaneously where Needed — Communicable through all Substances — Can be imparted any Distance — Its Rate of Progress.

THE nerves are the appointed and natural conductors of the peculiar force, that is generated in the brain and spinal column, to the various parts and organs of the body. By dividing the nerves, so as to interrupt this communication with the cerebral centres, the functions of the organs are at once suspended. This nerve-force is, therefore, essential to their physiological movements, and to the discharge of their office in the animal economy. The agent employed in producing the phenomena of what is called magnetism is either identical with the nerve-force, or is analogous to it, and is, also, conducted to the organs through their appropriate nerves, and affects their vital movements. It was formerly supposed that the nerves transmitted a subtle fluid called the animal spirits, and, subsequently, the nerve-aura, which flowed along their course to the different organs, analogous to the mode in which what was supposed to be an electrical fluid was conducted along the wire. But the fluid theory has been abandoned in explaining the phenomena of electricity, and also in physiology, in illustrating the functions of the nervous system. The new doctrine of force is now introduced into physiology, as well as into the science of the imponderable agents of heat, light, electricity, and magnetism. The idea of a nerve-aura, or fluid, is exchanged for the more satisfactory and rational one of a vibratory force that is transmitted by the nerves to the organs, in the same or similar way in which an undulatory wave is transmitted through the telegraphic wire. Bear in mind that the nerve-force and vital magnetism are the same, and the nerves are the proper conductors of both. Oftentimes you can affect an organ through the nerve leading to it better than by placing the hand in immediate contact with the part. The morbid state of an organ may be, and often is, the result of an abnormal state of the nerve quite remote from the organ itself. The negative swelling of the feet, the ankles, and the calves of the leg, is often caused by a congested and strangulated state of the large nerve in the hip, called the sciatic nerve, and, also, of the nerve accompanying the femoral artery. By removing the inflamed state of the nerves in the hip and in the inside of the thigh, the lameness and swelling in the limb below come right of their own accord. In this way I have seen a limb restored, in five minutes, that was so sensitive and powerless that it could not be moved. The foot may be sensibly affected also, by transmitting the psychic and magnetic influence to it along the sciatic nerve in the thigh. We know that pressure upon the trunk of a nerve affects the sensation of the parts to which it ramifies, however distant they may be from the place of pressure. When pressure is made upon the sensory and motory nerves of the lower extremities, as in sitting in one position for a length of time upon a hard bench, we experience in the foot the peculiar sensation called going to sleep. It affects both its motion and sensibility. By a slight blow or pressure upon the ulnar nerve in the elbow you feel a sensation, which all understand, in the little finger and on one side of the ring finger.

In a way analogous to this, you can transmit a magnetic influence to the various organs of the body through their appropriate nerves, which are a sort of telegraphic wire. He who makes use of Medical Psychology, for the cure of disease, should be so fully acquainted with the anatomy and physiology of the nervous system, that he can affect any painful or diseased part through its nerve conductor. Knowledge, here especially, will be power. He should be as familiar with the subject as he is with the alphabet. To illustrate what may be done in this way, if you wish to relieve that painful affection, neuralgia of the face and teeth, sometimes called *tic douloureux*, it will be of little use to apply the hands to the face. The pain in the face and teeth is an effect; the cause is in the state of the trifacial nerve, the fifth pair of cranial nerves. This is one of the largest of the cranial nerves, and is divided into three branches, one going to the eye, forehead, and nose, which are often affected in the disease mentioned above; and another going to the upper jaw and teeth, while the other branch is distributed to the ear, the tongue, and the teeth of the lower jaw. By wetting the finger in water, and placing it in the hollow just back of the tip of the ear, and cooling the inflamed state of the nerve there, you will often relieve, in one minute, the most excruciating neuralgic pain of the face and teeth. You thus remove the cause, and the effect ceases. It is always easy to do anything we know how to do.

The eye may be affected through the optic nerve, the second pair of nerves proceeding from the brain. It passes from the interior of the cranium, through an opening in the base of the skull, called the *foramen opticum*, to the cavity for the eye. It pierces the coats of the eye and is expanded upon the retina. It is disease of this nerve which occasions the gradual loss of sight called *amaurosis*, or *gutta serena*. It is a loss of power in the nerve, for which the psychopathic treatment is the best remedy. In its first stages, before the complete paralysis of the nerve, it restores its healthy tone, and sometimes opens the eyes of the blind. In painful inflammations of the eye there is a tender spot half way between the ear and the angle of the eye. A slight pressure here will be painful. By wetting the hand in water and applying it there, so as to cool the inflamed nerve, the inflammation of the eye will subside and disappear as if by magic. I have seen the most painful inflammation of the eye fully relieved and cured, in less than five minutes, by this simple treatment. You remove the trouble from the root. Remedies applied to the eye itself have but little effect. You must remove the cause in the abnormal state of the nerve, and then the effect will cease of itself. This is a general law, of which we should never lose sight.

The seventh pair of nerves, called *portio mollis*, enters the hard portion of the temporal bone, at the internal auditory opening, and is distributed upon the internal ear. You may affect the nerve of the ear just back of the zygomatic process of the temporal bone. Magnetism applied here will restore the hearing, sometimes instantly, where the deafness is occasioned by a loss of power in the nerve. Where there is an inflamed state of the membrane of the tympanum I have known it to be removed, and also the loss of hearing resulting from it, and likewise *otalgia* or ear-ache, by applying the magnetism of the hand wet in water just in front of the ear, at the angle of the *superior maxillary*, or upper jawbone. This will frequently relieve the trouble at once.

One of the most important nerves for the use of the psychopathic physician is called the *pneumogastric* nerve. It seems to be the nerve through which the mind acts upon every organ of the body, by which we may convey a mental stimulus to them, and thus affect the action of their involuntary functions. This office has been assigned to the great sympathetic; but this influences the involuntary processes of organic life, while through the pneumogastric nerve our will-power may modify the action of the internal organs, and send a spiritual force to the stomach, or liver, or kidneys. It constitutes, with its numerous branches and ramifications, a complete system of telegraphic lines, through which the mind of the patient, when in the impressible state, may affect the physiological action of any organ in the body. Through this nerve the mental and magnetic force may also act upon any part of the organic structure. The pneumogastric nerve is peculiarly adapted to this magnetic telegraphing. It proceeds directly from the brain through the *foramen lacerum*, the opening for the jugular vein, and is the tenth pair of cerebral nerves. It is widely distributed, sending branches to the larynx, pharynx, œsophagus, lungs, spleen, pancreas, liver, stomach, and intestines. From its wandering character, it was formerly called the *par vagum*. No telegraphic system could be more complete or better fitted for the use of the magnetizer. By placing the hand on the neck back of the angle of the inferior maxillary or lower jaw-bone, you are sufficiently near it. From this point you can affect any organ in the body and in any way you please, by directing your silent will-force to the place, and calling the attention of the patient to the part you wish to affect. In this way you can modify the action of the stomach, or the liver, or the respiratory organs, or the bowels and pelvic viscera. You can increase or diminish vital action. You can even warm the feet, or allay inflammation in any part. In a few minutes you can so affect the action of the skin as to throw the patient into a gentle perspiration, and cure an incipient fever. Through this important nerve, especially if the patient is in the impressible condition, you can produce any physiological effect at will. All these phenomena I have witnessed, and produced, a hundred times. They are not to me theoretical speculations, but demonstrated and accomplished facts. Where there is a lack of vital force in any organ, it is rendered negatively receptive, and when your hand is applied to the pneumogastric nerve, it attracts to itself your living magnetism thus imparted. It appears to act from a kind of instinctive preference, and the influence goes where it is most needed, without any effort of will on your part to give it direction. It goes to the weakened and negative part as spontaneously as water runs down an inclined plane. But the psychic and magnetic force which goes forth from you is a part of your living self, and is always under the control of your volitions. You say to it, Go, and it goeth. It obeys the silent or expressed command of your volitions. It passes, like a disembodied spirit, through all known substances, without apparent obstruction. The clothing does not isolate the patient, in the least, from its subtle influence. A person may be made to feel the influence of the hand, when it is not in contact with him, but held several feet away. The ordinary clothing worn by a patient is no obstruction to its effective application. It can be communicated from one person to another independent of spacial distance. I have made experiments with it at a distance of more than four hundred miles, and at lesser distances hundreds of times. Like spirit itself, it seems to be free from all material limitations.

It is worthy of remark that the nerve influence, or the peculiar force which the nerves communicate to the various organs, is not transmitted with the almost instantaneous rapidity of light and electricity, but requires time in sending it to an organ through the nerve, proportioned somewhat to the degree of sensitiveness of the patient. In sending an influence to the feet to warm them, the subject will be able many times, in his consciousness, to trace its progress as it passes along the route until at length it is felt in the loins and sciatic nerve, from which it soon reaches its destination in the lower extremities. And what may seem to some remarkable, the operator himself can often trace its progress in the patient by his own sensations. This many persons will confirm by testimony drawn from their own experience.

CHAPTER XVI.

THE AGENT IN THE PSYCHOPATHIC TREATMENT, AND ITS RELATION TO THE VITAL FORCE.

Theory of Mesmer — Discoveries of Reichenbach — The Odyllic Force — The Human Body a Magnet — Crystals — Chemical Action — Friction develops the Odyllic Force — Influence of Magnets on the Body — Experiments of the Author — The present Theory of the Imponderable Agents — Two Agencies concerned in the Phenomena of Vital Magnetism — The Physical Element — The Psychological — Their Relative Value — Proof that the Mind is the Principal Agent — The Ultimate Root of Disease — Influence of the Mind over the Body in the Impressible State — Therapeutic Value of Magnetism — Its Proper Name.

WHOEVER administers medicines for the cure of disease ought to have some adequate knowledge of the chemical nature and properties of the substances thus employed. So, in the practice of Medical Psychology as a therapeutic agency, it is well to possess, some understanding, some definite idea of the nature of the subtle agent which is the cause of the remarkable phenomena so often witnessed, and which has been demonstrated to possess such sanative virtue. It was the theory of Mesmer, who, though not the discoverer of animal magnetism, revived the practice of it, and was the means of calling the attention of the scientific world to it, that the magnetic sleep was produced by a subtle fluid universally diffused through space, being the medium of a reciprocal influence between the celestial bodies, the earth, and living beings. If this were true, and there can be little doubt that there is a basis of substantial fact in the hypothesis, it would account for the influence the heavenly bodies have ever been supposed to exert upon mankind and their destiny. The phenomena of gravitation and chemical affinity here find their explanation also. It would have been equally true, and, in fact, a higher verity, if he had taught that by means of this subtle agent the realm of spiritual existences could exert an influence upon those in this lower plane of life; for magnetism, in its wide extent and varied applications, is the science of the spiritual world. Mesmer also taught that this subtle agent insinuated itself into the substance of the nerves upon which it had, therefore, a direct operation; it was capable of being communicated from one body to another, both animate and inanimate, and that at a considerable distance without the intervention of any intermediate substance, and exhibited in the human body some properties analogous to those of the loadstone or artificial magnet. From this latter circumstance he gave the name of animal magnetism to it, which it has ever since retained.

The Baron Reichenbach, in his researches and experiments in magnetism, discovered by means of his sick sensitives, or partially developed clairvoyants, that magnets and crystals emit rays of a mild and beautiful light, which were visible to certain persons, both those diseased and those in health, in a *totally* darkened room. The flame from a horseshoe-magnet of ninety pounds' force was three or four feet in length. This newly discovered force, which he denominated *odyle*, was supposed to confirm the theory of Mesmer. He also ascertained that a similar flame streamed forth from certain parts of the human body, especially the hands, the pit of the stomach, the eyes, and the lips or mouth. This influence was supposed by him to be identical with that emanating from magnets, and to have an important relation to the vital force. But we are to bear in mind that this newly discovered force is not magnetism, but only associated with it, though distinct from it. This odyllic force was exhibited by magnets, crystals, plants, and in some degree by all material substances. It was found to be developed by electricity, galvanism, heat and light, as also by friction and all chemical changes. And this fact may account for the influence all these agents have upon the vital force. It was developed by combustion, the combination of an acid and an alkali, and all the subtle chemical changes going on in the human body. He supposed it to be the agent in animal magnetism, a view that met the concurrence of Dr. Gregory, and has been widely adopted.

There is no doubt that magnets exért an influence on the human body. Mesmer asserted this, and Reichenbach proved it. I have myself demonstrated this with a magnet of about seventy-five pounds' force. When passes are made with it, similar sensations are produced as when the hand is employed. Even the magnetic sleep may be induced by it. As a therapeutic agent I have found it far more valuable than the electro-magnetic battery. When passes are made with it, the influence of the hand is combined with it, and intensifies the effect. It may be employed as a useful auxiliary, sometimes, in reinforcing the influence of the operator. But many patients do not like it, and some feel a repugnance to it. It seems to them, to use their own expression, a coarser kind of magnetism. It lacks the more subtle psychological or spiritual element. I met with one extremely nervous and sensitive patient, who could not bear to have it disarmed in the room. It well-nigh threw her into convulsions. There are cases where its influence is grateful, and operates favorably.

No doubt the discovery of the odyllic force was a step in the right direction towards a correct apprehension of the nature of the agent producing the phenomena of magnetism. But it required the new doctrine of force, recently introduced into science, to fully explain it. The fluid theory has now been discarded, as inadequate to explain the phenomena of the imponderable agents. Everything is now explained by the theory of undulation or vibration. It is even introduced into both physiology and psychology. Whether the varied phenomena of heat, light, electricity and magnetism are produced by the undulation of a different medium, or are only the different vibratory movement of the same universally diffused medium, is not positively settled.

It is my own opinion, that in the phenomena of animal magnetism, both those exhibited in the ordinary experiments with it, and the sanative results of its employment in healing the sick, two distinct agencies are concerned, — the one material or odyllic, the other psychological or spiritual. Both are necessary to the highest results, but are not of equal value. They may be combined in different degrees in the organization of the operator. If a person has, in ever so large a measure, only the physical or material element and influence, but lacks the mental and spiritual force, he will accomplish but little in the cure of disease. For the gift of healing is more a spiritual endowment than any mere material and physical force, like that exhibited by the magnet or the galvanic battery. The material element may not be unimportant; it certainly is not so; but it is not the chief thing. For an animal, as a horse or a dog, may exhibit to a sensitive the odyllic flame, and they may impart an influence that may favorably affect the vital force and produce sanative results, as has been proved by experience, but they lack the spiritual element. There is no doubt that man can magnetize animals. We see hundreds of exhibitions of this. Animals may also magnetize human beings. But a good practitioner of magnetism, as a curative agency, must possess something more than *animal* magnetism. One proof that the mind is the principal agent is found in the fact that when one is in a state of great mental exaltation his magnetic power is largely increased. The greater the augmentation of our mental and emotional excitement, if it be of an elevating character, the more marked will be the phenomena produced. He who has the highest degree of psychological force, and possesses the greatest tact in managing and controlling the mind of a patient, will be the most skilful and successful in curing disease. The ultimate root of every morbid condition of the organic functions may be traced to a disturbance or inharmony of the spiritual nature in man, and of the vital force, an immaterial and imponderable principle. Disease being in its primary cause, imponderable and spiritual, a psychological force is best adapted to its radical removal.

The idea of a nervous or magnetic fluid must be given up, and the sooner our minds are freed from it the better. There may be a nervous force, but it is a force, and not a fluid. Neither the nerves nor the muscles are a force, but the instruments of a power distinct from themselves. The brain and nerves are the organ of the mind, or the medium through which a spiritual force acts upon and into the material organism, and influences its functional activities. In the magnetic state, the conscious impressible condition, the patient's mind or spirit, acting through the brain and nerves, may affect any and every organ in the body; and the mind of another person, either in this or another world, may aid in producing and intensifying the effect. Mind or spirit is the ruling principle in the bodily organism, and in all nature. It is the only causal agency. The changes of matter are only passive effects. Some spiritual force is the primal cause. What we call nature, the world, the universe, is animated by an all-pervading, ever-present spiritual life, which is the unseen cause of all its visible phenomena. Spirit is everywhere the life of matter, and the force underlying all its movements, in the earth beneath and the heavens above. In the cure of disease by the psychopathic treatment, we should have a boundless confidence in spiritual aid, and an undoubting faith in the power of mind over matter.

Whatever view we may take as to the nature of the subtle agent which goes under the name of animal magnetism, there is no room to doubt that it sustains an intimate relationship to the vital force, and must from this circumstance, when its laws are better understood, become the great remedy for disease, if not supplanting, yet taking precedence over all others. I prefer to call it by the more appropriate name of vital magnetism. But the name is not a matter of weighty importance, if it be at all appropriate and expressive of its nature.

CHAPTER XVII.

INANIMATE OBJECTS AND THEIR USE IN THE CURE OF DISEASE.

Communication of the Psychic Influence to various Substances — Their Influence upon the Psychometer — Amulets and Charms — Case treated by Dr. Gregory with a pair of Gloves — Influence of an Autograph Letter — Water a Conductor and Retainer of the Psychic Force — Testimony of Gregory — Experiments of the Author — How to Communicate it to Water — Its Peculiar Taste — Opinion of Deleutze — A Statement of Facts — It can be made to Produce the Specific Effects of any Medicine — A Physician's Mental Sphere affects the Operation of his Medicines — The Power of Suggestion — Effect of a Homœopathic Pill — Suggestion more Potent than Drugs — Case in Boston — Irrationality of Drug Medication — Substitute for it — Self-Limitation of Disease.

IT has been found that the odyllic and psychic influence may be imparted to various inanimate and inorganic substances, which will retain it for an indefinite length of time. Our clothing, the houses we dwell in, the beds on which we sleep, and every object we handle, or that comes in contact with our persons, as has been before remarked, is impregnated with our bodily and mental effluvia. This emanating sphere pervades, and, as it were, animates these otherwise inanimate objects with our physical and spiritual life. And when held in the hand by a good sympathetic clairvoyant or psychometer, they affect him with our states, and give him a perception of our character, even after the lapse of many years. We leave the impress of our life upon everything around us, and the psychometric sense is adequate to read the record. Various objects may be so pervaded with our psychic influence as sensibly to affect another person, especially when in the impressible state. This is the philosophy of amulets and charms. Their influence, after having been charged with the psychic and odyllic force of another, is far from being wholly imaginary. It may be as real as any of the phenomena of chemistry. These objects, worn about the person, exert a secret, and sometimes, in the case of persons of much sensitiveness, a powerful influence. Dr. Gregory mentions the case of a lady whom he treated for some disease, and who afterwards removed from Scotland to Paris. While residing in the latter place he was accustomed, once in a few days, to magnetize a pair of gloves and send to her. When she put them on, their influence would soon induce the somnambulic sleep, and as effectually as his own presence could do it. This might be pronounced the effect of imagination, had he not sent her occasionally a pair that he had not previously charged with the psychic influence, and although she was not aware of this fact, they produced no effect. This established in his mind the reality and positive nature of the influence. Various substances may be used for this purpose. A letter written to a patient is highly charged with a psychological force. It produces a sanative influence, sometimes far beyond that of any medicine. It is pervaded with the life and soul principle of the writer. It is the best substitute for the personal presence of the physician himself. It opens a living sympathetic communication between the patient and his medical adviser. But of all known substances, water seems to be the best adapted to this use. It is, at the same time, an excellent conductor and retainer of the psychic influence. The peculiar agent which is concerned in the production of the phenomena of Medical Psychology exhibits an affinity for water. This fluid is easily charged with the subtle force, and holds it for a long time. Mesmer asserted that water could be magnetized, but the idea was met with ridicule, — the fate of nearly all new discoveries. The experiments of Reichenbach confirmed the truth of it, and placed it on a scientific basis. And the late Dr. Gregory affirms that he has seen effects produced by magnetized water, that he should have deemed incredible if they had not taken place under his own observation. In the early part of my practice, the idea of producing any medicinal effects by water, otherwise than by the modes in which it is so efficiently employed in the water-cure, seemed extremely absurd. But at length I instituted a series of experiments with it, continued through a year, which it is needless to take time in detailing, but which soon convinced me that marked effects could be produced by its use, both upon those whom I had previously thrown into the impressible state, and upon those whom I had not. The results of these experiments led to the conclusion that it might be made a useful auxiliary in the cure of disease by the psychopathic method.

To charge a tumbler of water with the psychic influence requires only a minute or two of time. This is as good as an hour. Place the glass upon the palm of the left hand, and bring the fingers and thumb around the sides. Then hold the palm of the right hand over the top, moving it occasionally, at the same time gazing into it, and directing your will-force to it. You will feel a sensation of heat in the hollow of the hand which is held over the tumbler. The fingers of the positive hand may be placed together and their points held near the water. This concentrates the psychic force of the hand into it. A magnet can also be employed, but the hand is to be preferred.

The taste of water charged with this subtle agent is easily distinguished from that which has not been affected by it. More commonly it has a taste as if it contained a solution of bicarbonate of soda or saleratus. It is sometimes sweet, or acid, or bitter. It was the opinion of Deleutze that it would exhibit the taste of the medicine which the patient needed. All this may seem to some exceedingly ridiculous and unworthy of investigation. To offset this it may be proper to remark, that there are a thousand things in the orthodox practice of medicine that are not only equally ridiculous, but dangerous besides, while the use of water psychologically medicated, like the infinitesimal doses of homœopathy, is entirely harmless. It is saying much in favor of any medicine that it will do no harm. I will state as a fact that I have made water to produce the specific effect of various medicines, and oftentimes to taste like them. It has been made to act like a narcotic, allaying nervous excitement, and inducing a healthy, tranquil sleep without any of the bad, reactive effects of morphine. It has been made to act as a gentle cathartic, unattended with the griping pain following the administration of podophyllum, and relieving long-continued constipation in a short time. A single dose has been known to effect a permanent cure. It can be made to act as a tonic, an emetic, a sudorific, a diuretic, an alterative, or a stimulant. It may be used instead of liniments, washes, lotions, and gargles, and employed in any way in which medicinal preparations are used. In fact, the will of the physician can give to it any direction he pleases, and cause it to produce any specific effect upon the mind or body of the patient. This will not seem wholly unreasonable, if we bear in mind that all material substances in nature, and those employed in medicine, contain an invisible or spiritual essence. In this lie their active properties and power of influencing the vital force. This subtle and imponderable sanative virtue may be controlled by the will, and imparted to water or other substances. Again, it is not improbable, but has the certainty of a demonstrated fact, that medicines are greatly aided in their effects by the mental sphere of those who administer them. To this is to be attributed no inconsiderable share of their influence. In this way, bread pills, water drops, and homœopathic pellets, have been attended with marked beneficial results. There is no doubt that what is called *suggestion*, that is, the announcement to the patient that a medicine will produce a certain effect, greatly aids its action. When threatened with fever, some years ago, a homœopathic practitioner left me a few drops of something that tasted exactly like pure water, but gravely informed me that in one hour I should find myself, without extra clothing, in a gentle perspiration. This prediction proved true, for I had faith in it. And this faith predisposed me to the result. Some years after I took the same again, and without the least effect. The conclusion was a rational one, that my faith made me whole rather than the medicine. There is a law here, with regard to the influence of a physician's psychic force over the medicines he prescribes and prepares, and the power of suggestion in giving direction to their operation, that is worthy of attention. Cases are known where medicines have been left, and the physician has informed the patient that a certain preparation would produce a particular effect, and even when the wrong medicine has been taken, it has produced the predicted results. I was informed of a case in Boston, where a physician left a preparation of morphine, informing the patient it would act as a sedative to relieve his pain, but the patient misunderstood the word for a cathartic, and, notwithstanding the medicine is powerfully astringent, his bowels moved three times before morning.

It will be a great blessing to the world, if Heaven ever reveals to earth any substitute for the nauseous and noxious drugs that are now employed in the practice of medicine. If we had never heard of the administration of active poisons for the cure of disease, and some one should come into our house, and propose to give our child a dose of arsenic, strychnine, corrosive sublimate, or prussic acid, to relieve it of its malady, we could not bring ourselves to consent to it. It would seem unreasonable, absurd, and perilous, and look too much like manslaughter. While we had often heard of persons being killed, both accidentally and intentionally, by the administration of poisons, if we were not familiar with their use as remedial agents, it would appear to us more absurd than the use of magnetized water. It is difficult to break up the long-continued habit of thinking, instilled into mankind from their earliest childhood, that it is necessary to *take* something for every ailment. No matter where the disease is located, the stomach must pay the penalty by receiving the sickening and disgusting compound. If one has a lame foot, or a swollen joint, there is no reason or justice in punishing the stomach for it. If the patient cannot be cured of the false notion that he must *take* something, nothing can be more harmless, and as experiment has proved, nothing more efficient, than magnetized water or some simple preparation charged by the physician with his psychological force. But these should be used only as auxiliaries to aid the desired result. A very large proportion of diseases, at least four-fifths, as Dr. Bigelow has shown in his excellent little work on the subject, come to an end of their own accord by a principle of self-limitation. The duty of the physician is to watch the changes through which the disease passes, and to aid if possible the reaction of the vital force against it. Nothing is better adapted to this end than the psychopathic treatment, combined with the necessary hygienic regulations. I affirm, in all truth and soberness, that there are a multitude of diseases, deemed of a serious character, any one of which I would rather have and let it run through its self-limited course, without interference and without obstruction, than to take into my system the standard remedies, in the shape of poisonous drugs, that are prescribed for them.

CHAPTER XVIII.

THE LAW OF SYMPATHY IN ITS APPLICATION TO THE CURE OF MENTAL AND BODILY DISEASE.

Mutual Sympathy between the Physician and Patient — Platonic in its Character — Sanative Effects of Sympathy — The Phenomena of Sympathy Exhibited by the Magnetic Sleep — Community of Sensation — Of Thought and Emotion — An Image of Swedenborg's Heavens — How Magnetism opens Communication with the other World — Cahagnet — Demonstration of Immortality — The Sleep not Necessary to the Existence of Sympathy — Application of the Law to the Cure of Disease — Necessity of Health and Happiness in the Physician — Sanative Contagion — Treatment of Persons at a Distance — Sympathy with Outward Nature — The Other World — Swedenborg's Doctrine of Correspondence.

ONE of the earliest observed and most obvious phenomena of the so-called magnetic state is the sympathy which exists between the magnetizer and the subject. This is to some extent mutual and reciprocal. It constitutes oftentimes the basis of a pure and enduring friendship, that ends only with life, and even that is not its termination. This, so far as my observation goes, is entirely Platonic, and has no relation to sexual distinctions, exhibiting itself as strong between those of the same, as of the opposite sex. This friendship sometimes rises almost to the Damon and Pythias type, is extremely beautiful in its manifestations, and proclaims the divine origin and character of magnetism. A genuine sympathy is to many invalids, in their consciousness of isolation from a cold and selfish world, a medicine of potential virtue, and what they most need. It touches the hidden springs of life. There is in many chronic patients a painful sense of isolation from the rest of mankind, a conscious separation from the general life, and an instinctive yearning and craving for the touch of the sympathetic hand of kindness, and of a pure, heartfelt love, that most will understand, though it is difficult to describe. The physician who best meets this inner want will be the most successful in relieving them of their diseased condition. He connects the sundered link between them and the universal life. They are put in communication again with the vital whole, the collective man. It gives efficacy to his remedies, of whatever character they may be, and to whatever school of medicine he may belong. In the case of many melancholic patients, the voice and touch of a living sympathy come like rain upon a withering flower.

In the somnambulic sleep, as also in the conscious impressible state, so great is this sympathy between the magnetizer and the subject, that there exists a perfect community of sensation and emotion, and sometimes even of thought, reminding one of what Swedenborg affirms of the heavenly world, that so great is the oneness of spirit in each celestial society, that there is a universal communication of ideas and affectional states, a fellowship of kindred minds. The wisdom and bliss of the whole is spontaneously imparted to each, while each imparts its good to all. Magnetism creates a fellowship of intellect and of feeling on a smaller scale, but analogous to it. A prick of a pin on the person of the magnetizer is instantly felt in the same place by the magnetized subject, and this even when the eyes are bandaged, or the operator stands behind the patient. Whatever he tastes, the other tastes. If he smells a rose, or any perfume, or anything of a disagreeable odor, the other experiences a like sensation of smell. This community of sensation extends to the sight. Whatever the magnetizer sees with the outward organ of vision or in thought, whatever mental picture he forms, as of a mountain, a mansion, or a beautiful landscape, the subject sees with the mental eye. The image is daguerreotyped upon his mental retina. In this way thought, and all mental images or ideas are transmissible from one mind to another. In harmony with this law, spirits and angels may impress their thoughts, and the images of the objective scenery of the spiritual world, and even their emotional states, upon the sensitive and receptive mind. The same law governs here as in the phenomena of magnetism. This great law of sympathy renders practicable, without any miracle, an open and satisfying intercourse with the higher range of life. And magnetism is the science that is to give the world the long-needed demonstration of immortality, — of conscious individual existence after death. Cahagnet accomplished more with his entranced subjects, whose vision was opened up to the higher realms, to place the doctrine of a future life on a scientific basis, than the preaching of eighteen centuries had effected. The world is getting tired of theories, of doubtful speculations, of hypotheses and guesses at truth, and longs for positive knowledge. Magnetism, in its varied application, and far-reaching extent, will bring the grand idea of future existence into the domain of positive science, and place it as a fact among the certainties.

Prof. Bush has well remarked, in the preface to Stilling's "Pneumatology," that "unexpected developments in this region have wrought a wide-spread conviction, not only that there is a world of spirits, but that it exists in a far closer proximity to the sphere of the natural or material realm than has been previously imagined. The influence of mind upon mind, the communication of ideas from one to another when the parties stand in magnetic relation with each other, and the occasional entire subjection of the one to the will of the other, has been established beyond a question; and in these phenomena it has not been difficult to recognize a preintimation of the mutual intercourse of spirits in the other life, and the possibility of that between the denizens of this world and the next."

The magnetic sleep is not necessary to the exhibition of the phenomena of sympathy. It is seen equally well in the conscious impressible state, and more or less in every degree of it. This law of sympathy has its application to the cure of disease. The more a person is brought under the psychic influence, the more he will sympathize with the mental, emotional, and physical states of the physician. The better states of the one will be communicated to the other, and become his permanent possession. Hence the importance of the psychopathic physician being himself well and happy. Then his emanating sphere will have in it " a sanative contagion," that will be life-giving and health-imparting. He will light the smoking wick of the patient's candle of life from his own well-supplied lamp, and without diminishing his own flame. Chronic invalids in their negative, devitalized condition, say to the physician, in the language of the virgins in the parable, " Give us of your oil, for our lights are going out." By a strict conformity to the laws of life and health, he ought to be able to respond to this yearning cry for help, and impart to them a vital magnetism that shall send a thrill of life to every department of their being. It will not diminish his own vital stock, but may even increase it. For it was a foolish idea of the wise virgins, that if they gave of their oil to supply the lamps of others, they would not have enough left for themselves. God gives life to all, and without diminution of his own vitality.

In harmony with the law of sympathy, persons may be successfully treated at a distance. Psychological force is communicable, without regard to distance of space. The laws which govern the transmission of spiritual states and forces from one person to another at a distance have been explained in the previous work of the author. The law of sympathy has a wide application, and has much to do in the happiness and misery, the health and disease, the good and evil, we experience. It may be pressed into the service of him whose life is consecrated to the noble work of curing disease and alleviating human misery. If we possess a sound and healthy physical organism, and a mind at rest in the calm happiness of an unbroken fellowship with the central Life, and in living sympathy with all that is good and true in the universe, we may be as a fountain of life to others, imparting from our abundant and overflowing stores to supply their vital poverty. The law of sympathy gives to the vital force the power of self-multiplication, without dividing and diminishing itself. It is communicated, but the same undiminished amount remains. And by this great law all living beings in the universe are bound together in the same bundle of life. Isolation would be death. Conscious sympathy with God, with nature, with angels and with men, is life and health and peace.

The universe is not a mass of dead matter; but is pervaded with a living principle. When we are in sympathy with outward nature, life is imparted to us by everything around us. We imbibe the living soul of things, the omnipresent life. When this inward adjustment to the harmonies and vital activities of the outward world is disturbed and destroyed, as in most chronic ailments of a nervous and melancholic type, the tie between us and the living universe is sundered. We experience the desolation of orphanage, no longer deriving nutriment from the bosom of mother nature. The aspect of the world without is changed, and our vital relation to it is modified. Our course is like the wearisome march of a soldier out of step with his comrades. His movement is no longer aided and impelled by the imparted force of the whole collective body of his fellows. It is one of the high uses of Medical Psychology to restore the patient to harmony and sympathy with external nature, and put him in communication with her living forces, so that all the organic movements shall keep step with the grand symphony of the universe.

The material and spiritual universes are not sundered from each other, like the hemispheres upon our maps, but are vitally connected by the law of corespondence, so that —

"Scenes of earth
And heaven are mixed, as flesh and soul in man."

Swedenborg's doctrine of correspondence, and Plato's theory of ideas, though not identical, bear a close resemblance. Both agree in this, — that the things existing in the heavens are the animating principle of things in the material world. The objects of beauty and grandeur, which are cognizable by the bodily senses, are but the imperfect realization and representation, and as it were, crystallization of a higher and diviner creation.

Throughout nature, the external exists from the internal, the lower from the higher, as the body from its indwelling spirit. Plato's ideas are not mere mental conceptions, but something vitally real, — the pre-existing types and images of material things. True science and philosophy, according to him, consist not in the observation of external facts and sensible phenomena, but in the knowledge of things in their spiritual causes. The objects of the higher realm of existence are the living soul of things in this world, and sustain to them a causal relation. Swedenborg teaches all this with more scientific clearness than Plato, and applies this correspondence between the material and spiritual creations to the interpretation of human language, and especially of those parts of the Scriptures which he accepted as the word of God. The spiritual world is not far off in the abyss of space, but is interfused with this, and we may come into sympathetic conjunction and communication with the general sphere of its life.

THE OTHER WORLD.

" It lies around us like a cloud —
A world we do not see,
Yet the sweet closing of an eye
May bring us there to be.

" Its gentle breezes fan our cheek;
Amid our worldly cares,
Its gentle voices whisper love,
And mingle with our prayers.

" Sweet hearts around us throb and beat,
Sweet helping hands are stirred,
And palpitates the veil between
With breathings almost heard.

"The silence, awful, sweet and calm,
    They have no power to break;
For mortal words are not for them
    To utter or partake.

"So thin, so soft, so sweet, they glide,
    So near to press they seem—
They seem to lull us to our rest,
    And melt into our dream.

"And in the hush of rest they bring
    'Tis easy now to see
How lovely and how sweet a pass
    The hour of death may be.

"To close the eye, and close the ear,
    Wrapped in a trance of bliss,
And gently drawn in loving arms,
    To swoon to that—from this;

"Scarce knowing if we wake or sleep,
    Scarce asking where we are
To feel all evil sink away,
    All sorrow and all care.

"Sweet souls around us! watch us still,
    Press nearer to our side,
Into our thoughts, into our prayers,
    With gentle helpings glide.

"Let death between us be as naught,
    A dried and vanished stream;
Your joy be the reality,
    Our suffering life the dream."

Mrs. H. B. Stowe.

CHAPTER XIX.

HOW TO AVOID EXHAUSTION AND IMBIBING OF THE DISEASED CONDITION OF THE PATIENT.

Why Magnetism has been named Pathetism — Mutual Attraction of the Magnet and Iron — Reciprocal Influence of the Physician and Patient — Sympathetic Effect of the Disease — Passivity better than Struggling against it — Sleep a Remedy for it — How Jesus sometimes Healed the Sick — The Effect of Fear — How to escape Contagion — Importance of Faith — The Treatment of Fevers and Contagious Diseases — How to Manage Self-limited Diseases — An Invariable Rule — Economizing the Nervous Force — Exhausting Side-work — To Magnetize a Patient need not be Exhausting — Action and Reaction — The Psychic Agent not a Fluid — To Use a Magnet increases its Force — Needless Expenditure of Will-Force — Calmness is Strength — Illustrations — Use of Water — Deep Breathing — Sympathy between the Sexual and Vocal Organs.

IT is through the law of sympathy, that what we call the vital force is communicable from one person to another. This great law of our nature plays so important a part in the various phenomena of magnetism, that it has received the somewhat appropriate name of Pathetism. One of the most distinguished practitioners of the science in the United States gave it that name, and successfully employed it in the cure of disease. But this was seizing on one of the prominent characteristics of the state, and making that give name to the whole series of phenomena, just as Mr. Braid of Manchester, England, called it Hypnotism, from the somnambulic sleep, which is another marked feature of the magnetic condition, though not a necessary and universal concomitant of it.

In the case of a bar of iron and the magnet, there is a reciprocal attraction and influence between them. The iron attracts the magnet, as much as the magnet the iron, if they are of the same weight. So in the psychopathic treatment of a patient, something analogous to this is seen to exist. There is a mutual and reciprocal influence between the two. There is here the same law of action and reaction. The physician communicates a sanative virtue and vital force, and is often to a greater or less degree affected in return with the diseased condition of the patient. Sometimes he finds it difficult to throw off this sympathetic influence, which may linger about him for days. It is perhaps better to make no attempt to throw it off, but to be entirely passive and quiet. To struggle against it will often only increase it. If he can be sufficiently free from anxiety and excitement to fall into a tranquil sleep for a few minutes, he will wake up entirely free from it. The morbid effect is only temporary and sympathetic, and, if it is not interfered with, will soon pass away of its own accord. Just in proportion as he is affected with the diseased symptoms of the patient, does he afford him relief. In this way Jesus, the Great Physician, sometimes effected his remarkable cures. "Himself took our infirmities, and bear our sicknesses." He bore men's griefs, and carried their sorrows, and by his stripes or bruises they were healed. This cannot always be escaped by the person who devotes himself to this method of cure. He may not always be sufficiently positive to repel disease, and cast it out, yet it need occasion him no alarm. The least fear of imbibing disease will render one more liable to it. For it is a law that faith in the favorable operation of any remedial agency, the undoubting expectation that it will produce a desired and predicted result, causes a tendency in the action of the bodily organs toward that result. So fear predisposes us to any morbid condition of which we are afraid. Persons who are free from all anxiety will expose themselves to the most contagious diseases without harm, while the least fear will render them receptive of the poisonous contagion and effluvia. It is in harmony with this law that practitioners of Medical Psychology are sometimes affected with the morbid state of their patients. When from their occasionally being acted upon in this way, they come always to fear it, or expect it, it renders them increasingly susceptible to such sympathetic influences. Their faith should be sufficiently strong to raise them above it, and render them positively repellant to all disease. If we have a faith that springs from love, and extends its roots into the divine life itself, every morbid condition will retire and retreat before it; while fear will attract it. The one is a positive, the other a negative state of mind and of body.

The various types of fever and highly inflammatory states of the general system, together with all contagious diseases, had better not be treated psychopathically except in their incipient stage, when they are seldom brought to the notice of a physican. Most of these diseases are what are called by Prof. Bigelow, self-limited diseases; that is, they run through a certain course, and medicines are not competent to break up this regular progress and uniform succession of changes. They had better be left to the unobstructed operation of nature. When once established, it is not possible, even if it were desirable, to limit their duration, and essentially change their course. They are often only a healthy effort of nature to expel from the system some antecedent morbid condition, and they will best accomplish this result when the vital forces are only assisted by some general hygienic regulations. The late Dr. Warren was asked what he deemed the best remedy for inflammatory rheumatism. His laconic reply was, "Six weeks." So of these self-limited diseases, the best prescription is a certain and definite number of days, with pure air and water, and a strict conformity to the laws of life and health. If the patient or his friends have not sufficient faith in nature to cure these cases, they may be treated with the magnet, or magnetized water, or even by the use of harmless medicinal preparations. Thus nature in the proper time will cure the disease, and perhaps the physician, who has been only a spectator of her restorative processes, will receive the credit. The original homœopathic system, the method of cure adopted by Hahnemann and his immediate disciples, was well adapted to this class of diseases. An infinitesimal quantity of any medicinal substance is one that is next to nothing, and it is self-evident could not have much effect for good or evil. Yet it satisfied the patient that he was *taking* something, while it left the natural reaction of the system against the diseased condition free to cure it.

It is a good rule to follow, that we should never attempt to cure disease by the psychopathic method when we are suffering from excessive fatigue and exhaustion. Besides the loss of our mental and odyllic force at such times, which will weaken our power to affect and control others, our negative state will render us increasingly susceptible to the influence of the morbid condition of the patient. We had better wait until our vital force is renewed and our exhausted powers are restored. The person who would be most successful in healing the sick by this primitive and apostolic method should not waste his nervous force in other directions, but so far as practicable consecrate his energies to this one end. He will need all his mental and physical powers in this sublime work. All exhausting side-work must be avoided. He must economize the expenditure of his nervous life. It is enough for one man or woman to do. It is a work that might fill an angel's heart, and filled a Saviour's hands. It is the sublimest mission to which a human being was ever called.

To treat the ordinary forms of chronic disease by this method is not necessarily exhausting to the practitioner, but may even be invigorating to his vital powers. In every act there is action and reaction, which are always equal. The necessary reaction from giving, from imparting, will cause the supply to be equal to the expenditure. It is a law of far-reaching extent, and as invariable in its operation as gravitation, that he who gives shall receive an equivalent for what he imparts. There is nothing supernatural in this, any more than in the operation of the general law of action and reaction. If the psychic force were a subtle fluid imparted by one person to another, it would be natural to suppose, that after treating a few persons, the physician would be himself drained dry, like pouring a quantity of water from one glass vessel into an empty one. It drains the one to fill the other. But this imponderable agent is a force, and not a fluid. It may be imparted and not diminished, just as a large magnet will impart its power to another equal bar of steel, which will permanently retain it, and yet the original magnet has lost nothing. In fact, the more a magnet is used in this way, the stronger it becomes. The same law of increase from use holds good in the practice of Medical Psychology. Force is indestructible. It can be communicated and not diminished. Heat is a force,— a vibratory movement and not a fluid. One lamp will light a thousand others, without lessening its own flame.

Some persons make too great exertion in the treatment of the sick. They strain every nerve and muscle, as if they were going to lift a mountain from the patient. This needless expenditure of the will-force exhausts them, and would just as much if employed in any other direction, as in running or lifting. We can walk for miles without loss of nervous energy, while to run only a few rods will cause fatigue. Disease cannot be cast out by main strength. No violent physical demonstrations are necessary. Let there be strong faith, perfect self-reliance, confidence in your ability, a calm trust in the aid of higher powers, and a steady concentration of the will-force upon the desired result, and you will be successful. No outward and violent exertions can be substituted for these. They are tiresome and useless, and actually defeat the end at which we aim, by the disturbance which they occasion in the psychic force. All the great forces in nature are silent in their operation. They make little noise or stir. Imitate in this respect the operation of the Divine power in the universe. We often see parents, who wish to control their children, using loud and boisterous language, as if they were issuing commands to an army. All violent, noisy outward demonstrations indicate a lack of willpower. Others, by a look, or a simple movement of the hand, or a single word charged with a calm mental force, bring them into submission at once, for children intuitively perceive that there is meaning in it, and a strong will-force behind it. The tap of Cæsar's finger awed the Roman senate.

While giving the psychopathic treatment to a patient, it is well to breathe deep and full, and drink freely of pure water. There may not be in this so much of Prof. Huxley's *protoplasm* or physical basis of life, as there is in raw beef and brandy; but there is more magnetic life in it. A deep, full respiration, and its usual attendant, a deep, rich, full volume of voice, is indicative of strong vital powers; while a short, quick, and feeble breathing, with a weak, cracked, and broken voice, is an unerring symptom of a devitalized state. By a deep and full inspiration, both in the physical and spiritual sense, drink in life from the all-surrounding and viewless air, and educate the patient to do the same. This is of more importance to most patients than all the medicines that ever were prescribed or invented to bless or curse the world.

All physiologists, ancient and modern, have noticed the sympathy existing between the sexual organs and the larynx and voice, not only during the healthy, but also during the pathological condition of these organs. They mutually act and react upon each other. This sympathy is exhibited in various ways. On the establishment of the age of puberty in males, the vocal organs undergo a marked change, the voice usually being lowered an octave, and increased in volume. In eunuchs the voice approaches in quality that of women, and the performance of castration at an early period arrests the development of the larynx, and perpetuates the clear and feminine voice of adolescence. To the sympathy which exists between the reproductive and vocal organs is to be attributed the unpleasant spasms and choking sensation in the throat of hysterical patients, and the inflammation of the mucous membrane of the larynx in nervous invalids of both sexes. An undue excitement and overworking of the sexual organism will weaken the vocal apparatus, and a habit of deep abdominal breathing will, in turn, give strength and a healthy tone to the organs of generation. It is the best known remedy for every form of sexual disease. It has been established beyond a doubt by Dr. Desgranges, of Lyons, that persons who are addicted to an abuse or over-use of the sexual organs are the most liable to inflammations of the larynx, tonsils, and throat. A complete aphony, or loss of voice, is sometimes caused by a prolapsus or ulceration of the uterus, and never can be cured until that condition of the generative organs is removed. All physicians have observed the sympathy which exists in women between the respiratory and vocal organs and the womb. Thus, during pregnancy, or the approach of the menstrual period, or at its cessation, many females, especially those of a nervous temperament, experience a more or less remarkable change in the voice. Taking the sympathy which exists between the vocal and reproductive organs as an established principle of physiology, it is evident that no remedy for the multifarious forms of sexual disease can be more natural or efficient than an erect attitude and full and deep breathing. It is a prescription invariably and universally applicable to all such cases.

REST.

"Rest is not fleeing
This noisy career;
Rest is the fitting
Of self to one's sphere.

" 'Tis the brook's motion,
   Clear without strife,
Fleeing to ocean
   After its life.

" 'Tis loving and seeing
   The brightest and best,
'Tis onward unswerving,
   And this is true rest."

CHAPTER XX.

POWER FROM ON HIGH, OR SPIRITUAL AID, NECESSARY TO SUCCESS IN THE CURE OF DISEASE BY MEDICAL PSYCHOLOGY.

What meant by Power from Above — How God Helps Men — Spirits and Angels the Mediums — Magnetism Reveals the other World — Connects us with it — Testimony of Gregory — Deleutze — Cahagnet — Townsend — Scientific Proof of Continued Existence — Prof. Bush — The Work Assigned the Nineteenth Century — Laws of Spirit — Stilling's Pneumatology — The Psychopathic Physician Needs the Aid of Higher Powers — Availibility of it — The Laws by which it is Communicated — Two Kinds of Operation — Obsession or Possession — Influence or Mental Stimulation — These Conditions Described — How to render Available the Forces of the Spiritual World — Mental and Spiritual Laws — Spiritual Christianity — The Central Idea of the Gospels.

BEFORE the apostles were allowed to go forth on their public mission of healing the sick, and proclaiming the higher truths of a new dispensation, an advanced stage in the development of the kingdom of God on earth, they were expressly commanded to tarry in Jerusalem until they should be endued with power from on high. This alone would qualify them for the work assigned them in the plan of Providence. After this spiritual baptism they were different men. They were invested with a new power. Their carnal, material mode of thought was made to give place to a clearer perception of spiritual things. The fleshly veil was removed from their minds, their intuitions were quickened, their interior senses were opened, and they came into conscious communication with the spiritual world. To be endued with power from on high can mean nothing less than the reception of an influence from the higher realm of being to strengthen and augment the action of their natural faculties. So far as the power to cure disease is a special gift to the individual, it is a call from God and nature to use it for the benefit of humanity, and there is in it a pledge also of divine aid.

But it is the ordinary method of divine communication with men to employ the intermediate agency of spirits and angels. This is a truth fully illustrated and confirmed by the historical records of both Testaments. And Plutarch long ago observed, that "one supreme Providence governs the world; and genii (or subordinate spirits) participate with him in its administration. To these genii have been given, among different people, different names, and different honor." In the Old and New Testament they are denominated angels. Spiritual influences come to us from a sympathetic connection and conjunction with the intelligences and powers of the inner or higher world. This is effected without a miracle, and in perfect harmony with the laws of our nature. If it be a fact, and there is no reason to doubt it, that the apostles of Jesus were made the recipients of an influence emanating from the realm above, which exalted all their natural powers to a higher range of activity, so as to render works easily practicable, which, in their unassisted condition, were difficult and even impossible, there is no reason why we may not be endowed with the same psychological and spiritual force, and from the same quarter. They were elevated, by this sympathetic conjunction with higher intelligences, from the low range of the fleshly mind, to a plane of the inner life bordering on the high activities of the celestial climes. But it was effected without any departure from the ordinary laws of mind. Magnetism is the science which puts man into communication with the spirit-world, and connects this lower and rudimentary sphere with the higher range of life and intelligence. How this is done, I have shown in treating on the law of sympathy. It has been noticed by all the writers on animal magnetism,— Deleutze, Cahagnet, Townsend, and Gregory,— that persons in the higher stages of the magnetic state find themselves in communication with the spiritual world. "They hold long conversations with spirits, to whom they often give names, and who, in many cases, according to their account, are the spirits of departed friends or relations. The remarks and answers of these beings, seen in vision, are reported by them. Some of them affirm that every man has an attendant good spirit, perhaps, also, an evil one of inferior power. Some can summon, either of themselves or with the aid of their attendant spirit, the vision or spirit of any dead relation or friend, and even of persons also dead, whom neither they nor their magnetizer have ever seen, whom perhaps no one present has ever seen; and the minute description given in all cases of the persons seen or summoned is afterwards found to be correct."

If there be a spiritual world, not remote from this, but sustaining important relations to the world we consciously occupy, and a vital connection with it, as the soul and body in man, it is at least possible, and highly probable, that these visions of the somnambulic and trance states may be solid realities, and not the baseless fabric of a dream. Here is opened up to us a source of evidence of the truth of future existence of more scientific value than all the dry essays and pulpit declamations respecting immortality that ever issued from the brain of the religious world through all the past centuries of its history. It would be natural to suppose, that, after the various sects of Christendom had been *trying* to prove the truth of immortality for centuries, without placing it on any solid or satisfactory foundation, they would seize with avidity upon the positive evidence of facts afforded them by the higher phenomena of magnetism. But, strange to say, they reject and spurn the only proof that is adapted to the scientific mind of the age. They prefer theories and metaphysical speculations to living facts and demonstrations. Prof. Bush, one of the best scholars and clearest thinkers of this or any age, was led to the belief of Swedenborg's disclosures respecting the spirit-world, by his investigations into the phenomena of magnetism. Thousands of others, many of them the highest intellects of the country, and occupying every social and political position, from the highest downward, are reaching a condition of satisfactory faith in immortality by a similar route. To demonstrate the future conscious individual existence of the countless millions who have once lived in this lower world, and the connection of that realm of spiritual intelligences with this, and the practicability of a reliable and satisfactory communication between the two worlds, is the sublime mission of the nineteenth century. The science of human magnetism is the torch by the light of which mankind will explore their way to an all-satisfying faith and positive knowledge of immortality.

In the magnetic condition, whether self-induced or otherwise, the inner selfhood becomes freed, in a measure, from the material limitations of time and space. All spacial distances are annihilated, and the partially emancipated spirit soars on the wings of thought and desire, across continents to distant realms, and sees and hears what is there transpiring. It may travel to the remotest worlds of space, and hold communion with their inhabitants. The curtain that is drawn between this and the ever-present spiritual realm, always to the higher nature of man tremulous and wavy, and only partially opaque, is withdrawn, and the interior man has converse with the dwellers on the immortal shore, by means of the *cogitatio loquens*, or thought-speaking, which there becomes an indescribable inward vocal utterance. In more normal states, we sometimes experience what Whittier so beautifully describes in the following lines:—

> " So sometimes comes to soul and sense
> The feeling which is evidence,
> That very near about us lies
> The realm of spiritual mysteries.
> The sphere of the supernal powers
> Impinges on this world of ours.
> The low and dark horizon lifts,
> To light the scenic terror shifts;
> The breath of a diviner air
> Blows down the answer of a prayer:—
> That all our sorrow, pain, and doubt
> A great compassion clasps about,
> And law and goodness, love and force,
> Are wedded fast beyond divorce.
> Then duty leaves to love its task,
> The beggar Self forgets to ask;
> With smile of trust and folded hands,
> The passive soul in waiting stands
> To feel, as flowers the sun and dew,
> The One true life its own renew."

There are certain persons who have the power of detaching or abstracting the mind or spirit from the bodily organism, and removing from the inner life the veil of sense, and then they come under the operation of the laws that govern spirit existence. These laws have been described in the remarkable experiences of Swedenborg, whose open communion with another world for twenty-six years was in perfect harmony with the nature of mind. Stilling also has briefly stated some of those laws. He says: "Space is merely the operation of the material organs of sense; out of them it has no real existence. Therefore, as soon as the soul forsakes the latter, all proximity and distance cease. Hence, if it stand in rapport with a person who is many thousand miles distant, it can impart knowledge, by an inward communication, and receive it from such a one, and all this as rapidly as thoughts follow each other. When the soul is separated from the body, it is wherever it thinks to be; for as space is only its mode of thinking (or as Kant has expressed it, a state of the intellect), but does not exist except in its idea, it is always at the place which it represents to itself, if it may be there."

Again he says: "Souls and spirits communicate their thoughts to each other through the medium of the will; when one soul wishes another to know any particular thing, the latter immediately knows it; the one reads it in the interior of the other, even as the somnambulist reads in the soul of him with whom he stands in rapport." (*Pneumatology*, pp. 220, 231.)

Let it be borne in mind, that every person has an internal and an external manhood. The one we call the spirit, the other the body. There are individuals who can, in a greater or less degree, sunder the connection between these two departments of our complex nature, and then they come under the laws which govern life in the spirit-world. Their inner senses are unveiled, they see and converse with spirits and angels, and are transported in spirit to remote distances, for space to them has no objective, but only a subjective existence. The law by which one mind impresses its thoughts and feelings upon another at a distance operates with more unobstructed force. They telegraph their thoughts to an absent friend, and there are not wanting many instances where they have actually appeared in person, and entered into conversation. This is done in harmony with some law that is not now very clearly understood. It has long been known that mind can act upon mind independent of material distance. Cornelius Agrippa asserts that man naturally and without any miracle may convey his thoughts in the twinkling of an eye to another, however remote he may chance to be. "This," he affirms, "I have known and often done, and so has Abbas Trithenius, professor of philosophy at Padua." Petrus Pomponatius, who was born in 1462, had contended before Van Helmont, who taught the same thing, for the power of what is called imagination, or by the force of the will, of one person to send forth an influence upon another. He even declares that inanimate matter may be affected by this influence. This latter phenomenon seems to have been witnessed by Dr. Ashburner in an experiment which he details in the "Zoist." (Vol. v., p. 272.) If incarnated mind can do these things, why may not spirits disrobed of mortality, and even Jesus and his angels, do as much and even more? Why may there not be, in harmony with the known laws of our spiritual nature, a mutual influence between the denizens of this world and the higher or inner realms, and a reciprocal interchange of thoughts and perceptions? It certainly would not be a miracle.

As the apostles were unfitted for the performance of

their peculiar mission without the Pentecostal influences, so no one can be fully prepared to heal the sick by the "laying on of hands," as it is popularly called, who has not come into a conscious vital communication with the higher range of life and receives assistance thence. He may do something without this, but only small results can follow his efforts. His natural powers must be reinforced by some spiritual aid foreign to himself. He must come into vital sympathy and communication with the Christ and the angel-world. In a word, to employ the expressive phrase which the religious literature of eighteen centuries has consecrated to the expression of the idea, he must be "endued with power from on high." This will augment his magnetic and psychological force, and be the sovereign remedy for exhaustion, and a perfect security against injury from imbibing the morbid condition of the patient. He will find in this sympathetic union with the world above a never-failing supply of spiritual life and psychic force.

It has been found that a person who has been thrown into the magnetic state will sooner magnetize another subject than the same person can do it in his normal state. His psychic power seems to be greatly increased. A person in a state of somnambulism, whether self-induced or otherwise, will communicate that state to others much sooner than he could if not in that condition. There can be no doubt that whatever the physical agent may be which is concerned in the production of the phenomena of magnetism, the action of the mind of the operator is the prime force, without which little effect can be produced. But mental or will-force is the same everywhere, whether it be the action of a spirit in the flesh, or a spirit disrobed of its mortal vestment. I take it to be self-evident, that whatever influence our minds can exert over another person, a spirit divested of its outward covering, and freed from material limitations, can also exert with equal if not still greater power. If your mind is competent to magnetize another person, for instance a chronic invalid, in order to cure him of disease, a spiritual being is adequate to magnetize you at the same time, and thus increase your power. This is the idea at bottom in the phrase being endued with power from on high.

All nations, in every age of mankind, have believed in the existence of a world of spirits, and their influence for good or evil over men in this earthly sphere. It is a universal faith, the creed of human nature. Their power to affect us may be exhibited in different ways. There are divers operations, but the same spirit. These may be reduced to two general classes. There may be actual control both of the mind and the body of the subject. This is called obsession or possession. The controlling spirit may be either good or bad, and the phenomena exhibited will be accordingly. We are protected from the control of evil spirits by one of the laws of magnetism, for, as we have before shown, it is well-nigh impossible to magnetize a person for a wicked purpose, and a state of goodness is psychologically superior to a state of evil. This complete invasion of the material organs, this supplanting of the individuality, is not confined to the operation of evil spirits, or those of a lower order. The prophets of Jewish history were thus controlled, so that they wrote and spake what they did not themselves understand. According to Plato, this was the case, also, with the distinguished poets of his times. But a more common, and a more desirable form of the operation of the spirit, is where there is no control or possession, but only *influence*. In this latter case, the subject's individuality is not suppressed, nor is there any interference with his ordinary consciousness, but his powers are stimulated to an increased activity and a loftier range. All his faculties are exalted in their action. His natural powers are reinforced by the emanative sphere of the superior intelligence. His intuitions are quickened. He is borne, as on the wings of the spirit, to a higher and diviner range of intellectual activity. Powers of the spirit which, in our normal state, are suppressed by the fleshly covering, or exist only in a chrysalis or latent state, are temporarily emancipated. The subject is inspired, becomes mentally perceptive, and sometimes prophetic, but all the time retains his consciousness and identity. His mental peculiarities are not annihilated, but exalted and put to their proper use. This is the aid we need, and may have, from Christ and the angel-world, in the cure of disease. It is all in harmony with the laws of magnetism which exhibits both classes of phenomena. The ordinary magnetic sleep answers to obsession. The conscious impressible state corresponds to the latter class of phenomena. The more sensitive one is to the psychic and magnetic force, the more easily he may thus be influenced by higher powers.

How may we be thus influenced by superior intelligences, and how may we render the forces of the spiritual world available for assisting our weakness? The apostles cured disease in the *name* of Jesus; that is, by virtue of a power or influence emanating from him. Jesus still lives, and is as accessible to us as he was to them. We may come into sympathetic communication with him, and we cannot do this too often nor too much. Others beside the apostles, in every age of the church, have healed "all manner of sickness and disease among the people" by a power professedly and actually derived from him. The law by which this was done is in operation to-day, and is applicable to any and all other spirits with whom we may be associated by the power of sympathy, and to whom we may be vitally joined by an affectionate remembrance and congeniality of thought and feeling. All spirit, from the Infinite Mind down through every grade of intelligences, is governed by the same laws in communicating with others. It is one of these laws that their presence and aid must be *invoked*, earnestly and sincerely. They will come at our call. Christ himself, many times and in various parts of the world, has unmistakably and consciously manifested himself to others according to his promise. He pledged himself, before he left the world, by putting off his mortal body, to *come again* to men. He has kept his word. He has often come in the glory of the Father, and with his holy angels. In another world the emancipated spirit, free from material restraints and limitations, is borne on the wings of thought and desire from place to place. To think of another, with a desire to be with him and enjoy his society, causes an actual presence and conjunction of that spirit. But the same law of mind or spirit operates here. In our inmost being we are spirits now, — spirits clothed with a fleshly robe, — and are as much in the spirit-world as we ever shall be; for that world is where our spirit is, which is already in it and a part of it. If we sincerely invoke the aid and presence of higher intelligences, they will be with us in obedience to the laws of their nature and existence. If we are in sympathy with good and wise spirits, that sympathy is itself a state of presence with them. In the realm of spirit, distance is more a *feeling* than an outward measurement. A similitude of feeling, a likeness of state, is nearness. This only waits the power of thought and desire to bring it to the grasp of consciousness.

In accordance with these laws, we may be endued with power from on high, and our natural powers may be greatly augmented by the forces and influences of the world of spirits. This is perfectly normal, entirely in harmony with nature, and no infringement of the laws of divine order. It is an essential element of a vital Christianity. Without it, religion degenerates into a dead formalism, a ponderous machine without an impelling power, a body without a living soul. It has been the vital element, the animating principle, of all religions in every age. The grand characteristic of Christianity, by which it is distinguished from all other religious systems, ancient and modern, is the guiding, controlling influence of what it calls the *holy spirit*, which seems to include not only the idea of the emanative sphere of the divine Life, received by the soul, but also has in it the conception of a vital communication with the general sphere of the world of spirits. It has been established by science that every object in nature, every animal, vegetable, and mineral substance, is surrounded by an atmosphere that is composed of the subtle atoms and essences that exhale from it. This may with propriety be called the *spirit* of the thing. Its existence has been demonstrated by spectrum analysis, which plays so important a part in modern scientific investigations. The rays proceeding from each object, passed through a prism and magnified, form a rainbow peculiar to it, and which distinguishes it from all other objects. So there surrounds every human soul, every spirit and angel, an emanative sphere of their affectional and intellectual life. This may be *felt* by those of sensitive organization, and is clearly discerned by the clairvoyant faculty of perception, and is often seen and described as differently colored light. This is no dream, but something substantially real. The emanative sphere of the divine Mind, transmitted to us through the celestial and spiritual realms of being, is the *holy spirit*, so often mentioned in the New Testament. The general sphere of the intelligence and life of the spiritual world is the vital essence of all things here below. It is the divine magnetic life of men and all things in nature. A conscious conjunction with that superior or inner realm of life and light, and revelation thence, together with an elevation and stimulation of all the faculties of the soul, was not a mere transient circumstance attending the first promulgation of the Christian system, and the privilege of the first public teachers by an extraordinary vouchsafement of the divine favor, but it constitutes the very essence of the religion of the Gospels, and is their central idea. Christianity, in its purity, — not the altered and degenerate systems that have appropriated the name, but which Jesus could not recognize as having only the remotest resemblance to his religious system, — is emphatically a dispensation of the spirit. Christ left no written creed, no arbitrary and invariable rules of life, no fixed system of external worship, no stereotyped form of ecclesiastical organization and government, but everything, as the profound Neander has observed and acknowledged, was left to be unfolded by the influence of the promised spirit. The written word, the outward letter of Scripture, is not presented as an infallible guide, but Jesus promised to send the Comforter, the Paraclete or divine teacher and advocate, to *lead into all truth.* And Paul declares, that " as many as are *led* by the spirit of God, they are the sons of

God." And "If we have not the spirit of Christ, we are none of his." This spiritual influence is given, " *to help* our infirmities," or to strengthen our natural powers; " to make intercession for us," or to inspire within us suitable desires and emotions in prayer; to bear an inward witness to our consciousness that we are children of God; to direct in duty, and to quicken and animate all our mental faculties and bodily powers. On extraordinary occasions, the followers of Jesus were " to take no thought how and what they should say, but it should be given them in that day what they ought to speak." Paul declares that our bodies are designed to be *temples* of the holy spirit, thus exalting and dignifying human nature, and making every man and woman an incarnation of the Divinity, and an inspired messenger of another world. This spiritual influence, which, as we have seen, is the animating principle of nature, was to extend its divine magnetism to the physical organism, imparting to it health and vitality. "If the spirit of him who raised up Jesus from the dead dwell in you, he that raised up Christ from the dead shall also quicken (that is, vivify, animate) your mortal bodies, by his spirit that dwelleth in you." Here is a universal and available source of sanative power, and a potential spiritual remedy for morbid conditions of mind and body.

We are taught, in the religious philosophy of Swedenborg, that the holy spirit and the word of God are one. By the word of God, in the first chapter of the Gospel of John, is meant the general sphere of life and intelligence in the realms above, the calm, tranquil, all-animating, all-pervading, loving and living light of the heavens. "This is the true light that illuminateth every man who cometh into the world." It is an impersonal influence, and not a divine or human individuality. This is the living word, the essential substance of all truth, the unerring guide of all souls who are admissive of it, the source of a present, conscious, and all-satisfying revelation. It was the reception of this by Jesus that constituted him the Christ, the anointed one, and a Son of God. Whoever is receptive of it is made thereby a son of God, as the Son of Mary was. "As many as received it, to them it gave power to become sons of God." (Jno. 1: 12.) The church has strayed from the system taught by Christ and the apostles, in making the dead letter of Scripture supplemented by their stereotyped creeds, their lifeless formulas, and arbitrary rules, the guide of men's souls. Thus the blind have led the blind, until all together have fallen into the ditch of materialism and sensualism. The real word of God is not a book to be read, but a spirit, an illuminating, animating influence to be received, the living light of the never-distant heavens, the crystal fountain of truth, from which the prophets and inspired men of all ages and climes have drunk. Were every book in the world annihilated to-day, the true word of God, the Logos of John and Plato, would still remain and be accessible to every mind who loves truth for its own divine self. To come into communication with this living light, which Swedenborg denominates the spiritual sense of the external letter, is what the spiritually-minded disciple refers to in the following passage of his first epistle: "Ye have an unction from the holy one (or principle), and know all things. The anointing which ye have received abideth in you, and ye need not that any man teach you, but the same anointing teacheth you of all things, and is truth and no lie." (1 Jno. 2: 20, 27.) Such is real Christianity. It is not a creed, nor a liturgy, nor an outward mechanism of worship, nor an organization, but a spirit received; and "where the spirit of the Lord is, there is liberty." If such is the essential element of Christianity, its fundamental idea, where are the Christians? In sundering the conscious vital connection between men's souls and the upper world the church has lost its power, and is like a plant in a barren soil, stunted and withered by a long-continued drouth, or like a once fruitful tree, but now dead at the root. The spiritual gifts, enumerated by Paul (1 Cor. 12: 1–11), among which was the power of healing, have disappeared, and instead of it we have a dry creed and a dryer ritual. Instead of a living, present inspiration, we have the thoughts and teachings of men who lived centuries ago carefully embalmed and preserved in the tomb of the dead past. Instead of the worship of God in spirit and in truth, in the sacred solitude of the heart, and wherever the soul can meet an omnipresent Deity, and on every point of the globe where the heavens meet and touch the earth, we have only a mechanical substitute for it. But there are indications, not to be mistaken, that the time is at hand when the remarkable prediction of the prophet, uttered more than twenty-five centuries ago, shall be more fully realized than it was in the first age of Christianity: "It shall come to pass in the last days, saith God, I will pour out of my spirit upon all flesh; and your sons and your daughters shall prophesy (or speak from a present inspiration), and your young men shall see visions, and your old men shall dream dreams; and on my servants, and on my handmaidens, I will pour out in those days of my spirit, and they shall prophesy." (Acts 2: 17, 18.) It was not the design of Christianity to sunder men's souls from a conscious conjunction with the light and life of the heavens. Such a result did not enter into the conceptions and the plans of its founder. This unnatural divorce between the higher and the lower realms of being will some time end. Then celestial light, life, and power will flood the earth. The living word will take the place of the printed page, and in the spirit, that descends from the opened heavens, God shall give the promised new testament to his people. "Behold the days come, saith the Lord, when I will make a new testament for the house of Israel and for the house of Judah. Not according to the testament that I made for their fathers, but this is the testament I will make for the house of Israel: I will give my laws into their mind, and write them upon their hearts. And they shall not teach every man his neighbor, and every man his brother, saying, know the Lord; for all shall know me, from the least to the greatest." (Heb. 8: 8–10.) The testament, the word of God, which is to be the guide of man, will not be an external book, but an inward light and life, opening upward into the serene depths of the luminous atmosphere of the angel-world. Then men will live so near the other shore that they can "scent the odorous gales that kiss the eternal hills of day."

EUTHANASY.

"We need no change of sphere
 To view the heavenly sights, or hear
The songs which angels sing. The hand
 Which gently pressed the sightless orbs erewhile,
 Giving them light, a world of beauty, and the friendly smile,
Can cause our eyes to see the better land.

"We need no wings
 To soar aloft to realms of higher things;
But only feet which walk the paths of peace,
 Guided by him whose voice
 Greets every ear, makes every heart rejoice,
Saying, Arise, and walk where sorrows cease.

"Visiting spirits are near;
 They are not wholly silent, but we cannot hear
Nor understand their speech.
 Our Saviour caught his Father's word,
 And men of old, dreaming and waking, heard
The breathings of a world we cannot reach.

"They mounted to the skies,
 And read deep mysteries,
While yet on earth they placed a ladder there,
 Like Jacob's, that each round should lead,
 By prayer outspoken in a word or deed,
The soul to heights of clearer, purer air.

"They saw no messenger of gloom
 In him whom we call Death, nor met their doom
As prisoner his sentence; but naturally, as bud unfolds to flower,
 As child to man, so man to angel —
 They recognized in Death the glad evangel,
Leading to higher scenes of life and power."

CHAPTER XXI.

MISCELLANEOUS DIRECTIONS IN THE TREATMENT OF DISEASE, INCLUDING THE METHOD OF A CORRECT DIAGNOSIS.

Sympathy between Different Parts of the Body — Use of the Law — The Arms and Lungs — Treatment of Pulmonary Diseases — The Relief of Pain — Inflammations — Reproductive Organs — Treatment of Female Diseases — Transient and Permanent Cures — Medical Psychology and the Swedish Movements — Simplicity of the Right Remedy — Illustrative Case — Sympathetic Clairvoyance — How Developed — Its Use in the Diagnosis of Disease — Importance of a Correct Diagnosis — Nature of Interior Perception — It is a Spiritual Gift — Its Sublime Uses — Reality of the After-Life.

THERE are certain parts of the body that are connected by sympathy, though they may be widely remote from each other. Paul seems to have had a shadowy, undefined glimpse of this law of sympathy in the action and state of the various organs and parts of the bodily structure, and refers to it in the twelfth chapter of the first epistle to the Corinthians. But his description is more poetic than scientific. The head and feet, being opposite poles of the living magnet, are mutually affected each by the state of the other. A good circulation in the feet indicates a cool, clear brain. When the head is hot and congested, the feet are cool. The arms and lungs exhibit the same sympathetic relation to each other. There is an actual nervous connection between them, through the brachial plexus. When you violently move your arms, as in swinging them, or in striking, the nervous thrill that goes to the muscles of the arm passes at the same time along the respiratory nerve to the diaphragm and lungs, and causes an increased breathing. The hectic flush in the cheek reveals a point in sympathy with the state of the lungs. When a person is in the impressible condition, the psychic force applied here will affect the action of the lungs. For inflammation and other forms of pulmonary disease, we may favorably affect their state, by stimulating the vital action of the arms by friction, pressure of the muscles, and kneading. The practice of kneading, rubbing, percussing and working the different parts of the body, anciently called *tripsis*, has a powerful effect in increasing their vital action, and promoting a vigorous circulation of the living forces through them. Such a treatment of the arms is an efficient remedy in pulmonary complaints. The life imparted by it is conveyed by sympathy to the lungs. In inflammation of the lungs, the stimulation of the arms acts as a derivative or counter-irritant. This kind of treatment seems to be a specific for the various forms of pulmonary disease.

Inflammations are sometimes best relieved, and most effectually cured, by exciting the parts below, especially if those parts are in sympathetic connection with the seat of the inflammation. The excitement of the parts below the inflamed organ acts on the principle of a counter-irritant, only in a more natural and healthy manner. In uterine inflammations, the calf of the leg will always be in a negative, devitalized condition, for this part of the lower extremities exhibits a special sympathy with the reproductive organs, equally marked with that of the breasts or mammary glands and the same parts, or the nipple and clitoris. In some uterine diseases the calf of the leg will be extremely sensitive to pressure, and sometimes the sensation will be analogous to that which is felt when the leg is said to be asleep, when it is touched or moved. In inflammation of the uterus and its appendages, and in prurigo of the vulva, and nymphomania, some physicians apply counter-irritants, as mustard or cantharides, to the calf of the leg. But the treatment above described, as applied to the arms for pulmonary complaints, when employed here, is much better than any counter-irritant, as it restores the parts to a healthy vital action, and determines the circulation of the living forces, and the accumulated magnetism of the reproductive organs, to the place in sympathy with them. It is nature's remedy for this class of diseases, especially in conjunction with the proper treatment of the abdominal muscles before described. When an organ is in a state of inflammation, or undue excitement, or exhibits an excessive accumulation of life in it, the part with which it is sympathetically connected will be in a negative or devitalized condition. By exciting the vital activity of this part, it attracts to it the surplus vitality of the organ, to which is added your own psychic force and magnetism, and thus the healthy equilibrium is restored.

Pain can be effectually relieved by holding the hands for a moment or two on the place that is the seat of the increased sensibility, and then placing them on some part below, and making passes downward. This attracts the influence imparted by the hand downward, and the pain with it. It is sometimes astonishing to the patient, how soon this apparently simple treatment will allay the most intense pain. In extremely acute pains, attended with a great degree of sensitiveness in the parts, it may assist to relieve it to wet the hands in water containing a little sulphuric ether. As the inhaling of ether produces a general insensibility of the nerves of feeling, so its external application produces a corresponding local insensibility. It may sometimes be usefully employed as an auxiliary to the psychopathic treatment.

Some troubles, which are usually treated by physicians of the regular school as local diseases, are most successfully managed by restoring the general tone of the system. There are but few, if any, strictly local diseases. Owing to the action of the law of sympathy, which connects the organs in a harmonious whole, if one part suffers, all suffer more or less with it. This is one reason why the magnetic movement-cure, by imparting the vital principle itself, is so efficient in the cure of disease. It is better calculated than any known remedial agency to restore the system to a vigorous tone, and thus remove all local morbid conditions. To improve the general health and vigor of the whole system is the best method of treating the diseases peculiar to the female organism, whose name is legion. They are usually what their own intuitions have so expressively named them, that is, " weaknesses." They result from a general loss of vital force, and the parts of the system which have a constitutional and hereditary tendency to debility and disease, are the first to be affected. It is evident that where this is the case, the remedy is to restore the general strength, which the system of Ling, in connection with Medical Psychology, is so well calculated to do. When the animal functions are generally healthy and performed with due vigor, local " weaknesses" soon disappear. This is the most effectual remedy for the long list of female diseases, the various forms of prolapsus, leucorrhœa, or disturbances of the menstrual function, chlorosis, hysteria, polypus, and ovarian tumors.

It should be the aim of the psychopathic physician, not only to cure a patient of his disease, and to afford him a temporary relief, — for this is only half his work, — but to show him how to keep well, and to give permanency to his recovery. Many otherwise efficient practitioners of the system fail precisely here. It is equally true also of physicians of all schools. The patient must be put upon the royal road of obedience to the laws of life and health. The practice of general hygiene must be insisted upon. His diet must be regulated according to the necessities of the case. He must have exercise or rest, as the peculiarities of the case may demand, deep breathing, pure air, proper attention to bathing and cleanliness, and be regular in all his habits. It is of little use to cure a patient of disease, and leave the causes of the morbid state in full operation. These must be eradicated, in order that the cure may be permanent. If this is not attended to, the patient will fall from grace, and his backsliding may bring the therapeutic influence of mental medicine into disgrace.

There are no two systems of curing disease which work better together than Medical Psychology and the Swedish Movement Cure. They are twin sisters, and mutually aid each other. Each borrows efficiency from the other. Every one who uses the first as a curative agency in the treatment of chronic diseases will do well to acquaint himself with the system of Ling, and the principles of the Movement Cure, as unfolded in the work of Dr. Taylor on the subject. This will be far better than dabbling with medicines of any kind. He should thoroughly study also the science of vital magnetism. One can gain a competent knowledge of the literature of the subject, by perusing the works of Deleutze, Gregory, Cahagnet, Townsend, the recent excellent work of Dr. Fahnestock on "Artificial Somnambulism;" and the previous work of the author of this, entitled the "Mental Cure," describing the mental aspect of health and disease and the psychological method of treatment. We should seek for light from every source, — books, conversation, our own intuitions, and communication with the general sphere of intelligence above.

The remedy for disease is often extremely simple, and its efficiency consists in its being the right thing, in the right place. An illustrative case will render this plain. Some years ago, I received a telegram urging me to go, by the next train, to a neighboring town, to attend a man dangerously sick. He had been suffering for ten days from gastric inflammation. Everything swallowed was instantly ejected from the stomach, even a spoonful of water. His condition was an extremely critical one. I perceived, by an examination of the case, that the pneumogastric nerve was inflamed and congested. This was the root of the trouble. The remedy was also suggested. An application of cloths wet in warm water, and pressed upon the back of the neck with the hand, and changed at brief intervals, relieved him in ten minutes. The inverted action of the stomach and bowels was changed at once, and the cure was effected. Only a general weakness remained, from which he soon rallied. By so simple a remedy, a man was raised from the verge of dissolution, in a few minutes, to health. The cure was effected in the presence, and with the approval, of a Professor of the Dartmouth Medical College. Many other cases might be given illustrating the same point,

— the simplicity and efficiency of the right thing, in the right time and place. There is an inseparable connection between the cause of a diseased condition and the morbid effects. A radical cure implies the removal of the producing cause.

Is there any sure and reliable guide, which we may follow, in gaining a knowledge of the nature and cause of the morbid state of a patient, and the proper remedy? The gift and art of healing, by this method, is usually accompanied with the power, the instinctive faculty, of doing this. The practice of Medical Psychology for a short time seems to develop the intuitive perceptions of the physician, so that he sees, at a glance, the diseased condition of a patient. He becomes more and more impressible, and sympathetically clairvoyant. This remarkable power is extremely accurate and reliable in the diagnosis or detection of the location and peculiar symptoms of disease. It is adequate to a correct diagnosis in every case, especially if there be with it an adequate knowledge of the anatomy and physiology of man, and the nature and symptoms of disease. Some clairvoyants, as they are called, are defective here. Their intuitive perceptions are acute and clear, and they can locate a pain or a diseased action, but know not even the name of the organ to which it belongs, or the disease of which it is symptomatic. There are some physicians of the regular school, who have gained great celebrity in the skilful diagnosis of disease, who do it in this way, and yet while they secretly practise sympathetic clairvoyance or psychometry themselves, are often too ready to ridicule it in others. Many have owned to me that they detect the state of a patient in this way more than by the ordinary mode of examining the pulse, the tongue, and the character of the excretions. The first step toward a cure is a correct diagnosis of the disease. To gain an accurate knowledge of the morbid state is half of its cure. Many a person has been doctored into the graveyard, by treating him for a disease he never had, and thus administering to him the wrong medicines. The blindness of the physician has quenched the light of life in the patient. Psychometry is of inestimable value in enabling the physician to ascertain the exact state of health of an individual, and in forming a correct judgment as to the origin, cause, nature, location, and present progress, of the most complicated and obscure diseases. When aided by medical science, it is a well-nigh unerring guide to a discriminating knowledge of disease, and the peculiarities of each individual case. We cannot over-estimate the importance and worth of this peculiar interior perception, with its delicate sensitiveness to the least diseased action in another person, its indescribable inward discernment of the hidden cause, and its intuitive flash of light as to the proper mode of removing it. This sensitiveness to the state of another may be compared to a delicate differential thermometer. The slightest changes of temperature, which our ordinary sensations are inadequate to perceive, are indicated by it at once. But sympathetic clairvoyance is not only an immediate response of our system to the feelings of another, but is also an acute perceptivity. It sees as well as feels. It is a spiritual light, a ray of a higher sun, and the development and disclosure of a hidden power of human nature, which does not ordinarily come to freedom and conscious activity in this first stage of our existence. It sympathetically feels the disease of the patient, and sees the cause, near or remote, and suggests by an intuitive flash the right thing to be done.

Interior perception, as Swedenborg denominates it, is a spiritual gift, in its highest forms of manifestation. I mean, by this, that a spiritual influence develops the dormant and latent power in human nature, and unveils senses that are suppressed by the fleshly covering. What is ordinarily called clairvoyance is only an imperfect imitation, and sometimes a bungling counterfeit of it. It is the concomitant of the "gift of healing." Among the *charismata*, or gifts of the spirit, enumerated by Paul, are mentioned the word of wisdom and of knowledge, or an exaltation of the intellectual powers to an extraordinary range of action, and the discerning or seeing of spirits. If this latter gift be interpreted to mean the intuitive reading of character, it implies nothing less than perception; for to read the secret thoughts of men, their past history, and present character, is one of its common functions. If it means, as it naturally does, the power to see spirits, then it certainly is an interior perceptivity that is indicated. The detection of disease by a glance, the intuitive reading of thought and character, and the vision of spiritual beings and things, are effected by the same power. The distinction is in its different range of action. The power of intuitive perception, which is innate in human nature, and belongs to its essence as one of the properties of our inner being, is unfolded and stimulated to activity by spiritual influences. The practice of Medical Psychology operates in the same way, and aids its development. The practitioner becomes more and more impressible. This facilitates communication with the higher realms. Impression, or thought-speaking, is the most desirable form of reciprocal converse and intercourse with the other world. He who is sympathetically impressible lives in speaking distance of another and better range of life, and its more exalted intelligences. By light borrowed from the living effulgence of that realm he will see the nature and cause of a diseased condition, both in its mental and physical aspects, and have an indefinable perception, intuition, or impression of the right thing to be done. The future science of the world will appreciate the worth of this wonderful gift, and educate and direct it to its proper sphere of use. It can be made to search out the hidden haunts of disease in the human system, or to explore the secrets of the worlds of space, or to disclose the sublime mysteries of another life, lift from it the veil of darkness, and demonstrate to the doubting, hesitating faith of the world the truth of immortality.

THERE IS NO DEATH.

"There is no Death! The stars go down
  To rise upon some fairer shore;
And bright in Heaven's jewelled crown
  They shine for evermore.

"There is no Death! The dust we tread
  Shall change beneath the summer showers
To golden grain or mellow fruit
  Or rainbow-tinted flowers.

"The granite rocks disorganize
  To feed the hungry moss they bear:
The forest leaves drink daily life
  From out the viewless air.

"There is no Death! The leaves may fall,
  The flowers may fade and pass away—
They only wait through wintry hours
  The coming of the May.

" There is no Death! An angel form
　　Walks o'er the earth with silent tread,
　He bears our best loved things away,
　　And then we call them — Dead.

" He leaves our hearts all desolate —
　　He plucks our fairest, sweetest flowers;
　Transplanted into bliss, they now
　　Adorn Immortal bowers.

" The bird-like voice whose joyous tones
　　Made glad this scene of sin and strife,
　Sings now in everlasting song
　　Amid the Tree of Life!

"And where He sees a smile too bright,
　　Or hearts too pure for taint and vice,
　He bears it to that world of light
　　To dwell in Paradise.

" Born into that undying life
　　They leave us but to come again;
　With joy we welcome them — the same
　　Except in sin and pain.

" And ever near us, though unseen,
　　The dear immortal spirits tread;
　For all the boundless universe
　　Is Life — There are no Dead!"

CHAPTER XXII.

INSANITY AND ITS PSYCHOPATHIC TREATMENT.

Different Forms of Insanity — Its Leading Characteristic — Analogy to Dreaming — Mental Condition in Dreams — Insanity and Somnambulism — Resemblance of the two States — Cerebral Condition — Mental Exaltation — Want of Recollection — Influence of the Bodily Organs — Delirium and Nightmare — Causes of Insanity — Not a Bodily Disease — Loss of Magnetic and Cerebral Harmony — Magnetic Exhaustion — Vampirism — Morbid Odyllic and Magnetic Sensitiveness — Obsession — Remarks of Dr. Abercrombie — Insanity a Peculiar Magnetic State — Adaptation of the Psychopathic Treatment to its Cure — Influence of Kindness.

THE peculiar mental and cerebral condition that goes under the general name of insanity exists in different degrees, and assumes various forms. When the deviation from the sound mental status and the divergence from the usual normal manifestations of mental action are only slight, it is called eccentricity. This is the lowest degree of an unbalanced or abnormal mental state, and is of more frequent occurrence than the higher forms of mental inharmony, which are denominated insanity. Where the hallucination is confined to one subject, and on all others the patient exhibits no deviation from the ordinary condition of a sound mind, it is called monomania. When the controlling false impressions or ideas are of a depressing character, it constitutes the abnormal mental state known as melancholia. This is often attended with a tendency or impulse to self-destruction. Where the ruling ideas are of a more exalted character, it is mania or madness. In this form of mental disease the lower passions and propensities sometimes break loose from all voluntary restraint.

The grand characteristic of insanity is the partial or complete loss of voluntary control of the thoughts, emotions and activities of the subject of it. It has been long ago observed by writers on insanity, that there is a remarkable analogy between the phenomena exhibited by it and those of dreaming and somnambulism. This is so obvious a fact as to force itself upon the attention of the most superficial observer, and yet is a truth of fundamental importance in deciding upon the best method of treatment, or that which from its adaptation to the nature of the disease promises the most certain curative results. The leading characteristics of both states are the same. Dr. Holland (*Mental Physiology*, p. 110) remarks, "A dream put into action (as in reality it is, under certain conditions of somnambulism) might become madness in one or other of its most frequent forms; and, conversely, insanity may often, with fitness, be called a waking and active dream." In dreaming, the peculiar condition of the mind may be expressed by two facts of consciousness:—

1. The impressions which arise in the mind and the images which float before the mental vision are believed to have a real and present existence; and this belief is not corrected, as in the waking state, by comparing the conception with the things of the external world. The subjective states of the mind have a predominating influence, while in our ordinary waking state the outward senses control our judgment and action.

2. The ideas or images in the mind follow one another

according to the law of association, over which we have no control, and cannot, as in the waking state, vary the series or change it at will. In all forms of insanity and the numerous modifications of mental disease, we shall see these characteristics of dreaming exhibited in a higher or lower degree. The higher forms of mania are a sort of dream from which the patient does not awake. To illustrate the remarkable analogy between dreaming and insanity, Dr. Abercrombie mentions the case of a maniac who had been for some time under the care of the celebrated Dr. Gregory, and entirely recovered. For a week after his recovery he was harassed during his dreams by the same rapid and tumultuous thoughts and the same violent passions by which he had been agitated during the period of his insanity. This is by no means a solitary fact, but is of frequent occurrence, and speaks volumes as to the true nature of insanity.

In a work on the Identity of Dreaming with Insanity, M. Moreau, of Tours, remarks: "There are many insane persons who trace their delirious ideas, or convictions, or hallucinations, to a dream. With many, insanity is in reality but the continuation of the dream. In confirmed insanity the dreams have effected such profound impressions upon the organism that they cannot be effaced by the waking condition. The impressions of dreams are sometimes so vivid that we find it difficult to divest ourselves of the idea of their reality. This is certainly a moment of insanity. In order that the insanity shall continue, we have only to imagine that the fibres of the brain have suffered too violent a shock to have recovered themselves. The same thing may occur more slowly."

Somnambulism, whether it occur spontaneously, or be artificially induced by magnetism, exhibits a still closer relationship and analogy to insanity. There is the same absence of voluntary control over the thoughts and feelings as in ordinary dreaming, and the same predominating influence of the subjective states of the mind over the outward senses. It differs from dreaming by the bodily organs being more under the control of the will, so that the subject sometimes converses freely on the ideas that occupy his mind, walks about, and even engages in manual labor. In somnambulism, which is a peculiar magnetic condition, the cerebrum, the organ of voluntary thought and life, is quiescent, and the patient lives and acts from the cerebellum, the organ of involuntary thought and activity. There are many insane persons in whom this cerebral condition is quite manifest, the forebrain being abnormally cold, as it is in long-continued sleep. This negative condition of the cerebrum, at least the anterior portion of it, will be found on investigation to be a quite uniform accompaniment of insanity.

There are many other facts which go to prove the analogy of insanity to somnambulism, if not the perfect identity of the two states. In somnambulism and dreaming there is often witnessed a great exaltation of the intellectual powers. The mind is elevated to a higher plane of activity, so that they perform deeds beyond their usual powers, and comprehend subjects beyond their ordinary grasp. This is true of insanity. The thoughts and feelings are often acute and intense, far beyond the normal state of the same persons. They are often more or less clairvoyant. Many cases of this have come under my observation. They sometimes see and even hear things transpiring at a distance, and the objects and persons of another and higher world are not unfrequently unveiled to their inner vision. How closely this resembles the phenomena of the magnetic state, no one can fail to perceive.

On coming out of the magnetic condition called somnambulism, and of ordinary dreaming, there is usually an entire forgetfulness of all that has occurred in that state, or only a vague recollection of it. How true this is of the higher degrees of mania, I need not point out to any one in the least degree acquainted with the subject. Persons subject to periodical attacks of insanity, on recovering have no recollection of what took place while in that state, but distinctly remember all that transpired when under the influence of a subsequent attack. In this respect the two states of somnambulism and insanity come together. I have seen persons in the magnetic sleep, who, if it had been found impossible to wake them up, and they had remained in it for any considerable length of time, would have been deemed proper candidates for an insane asylum, when they were in no proper sense insane at all. They were only in another, and perhaps higher mental condition, the laws of which are not fully and generally understood. There can be little doubt that our asylums are crowded with persons in a similar state, and who by a judicious psychopathic or magnetic treatment might be restored to a normal intellectual condition.

Dreams are often greatly influenced if not occasioned by the condition of the bodily organs. The same is true of the hallucinations of insanity. The monomania of De Quincey, which consisted in the impression that he carried a hippopotamus in his stomach, probably arose from the peculiar condition of that organ resulting from opium-eating. The violent ravings of maniacs, and their ungovernable propensity to destroy everything within their reach, is attended with an inflamed and over-sensitive state of the mucous surface of the stomach and duodenum. The peculiar condition of the uterine organs that underlies the pleasing visions and beautiful waking dreams of some forms of hysteria, without doubt, gives character to the condition of many insane patients. Between the fearful visions of delirium tremens and nightmare there is a close analogy, and both are due to the condition of the digestive organs. In delirium tremens the fore-brain is often cold, while the part of the cerebrum in sympathetic connection with the stomach and bowels, and which is in close proximity to the organ of cautiousness, is much inflamed and congested. The phenomena of dreaming and the mental manifestations in somnambulism receive direction from, and bear the stamp of, the dominant propensities and characteristics of the individual. These frequently constitute the basis of the disordered mental manifestations of the insane. I need not trace further the analogy between insanity and the somnambulic state. The fact of their analogy or identity, if once established, must be the foundation on which to erect a more rational and efficient theory for the treatment of this unfortunate class.

The causes of insanity are various. Attempts have long been made to refer it to bodily disease, but this is seldom satisfactory, as there are many cases where the various bodily organs are but slightly disturbed, not more so than in people in general who are not insane. I do not deny that disease of the body is often associated with it. Constipation of the bowels is a uniform attendant of it, especially of melancholia. There is often a change in the relative proportion of the various chemical constituents of the body, as an excess of phosphorus in the brain. The frontal sinus may be found partially closed or contracted. The excreting organs, as the skin, the liver, and the kidneys, may be obstructed in their functional action, and the spleen enlarged. But whether the pathological condition is to be viewed as cause or effect is an open question. It may be only the resultant of the antecedent mental disturbance and inharmony. Certain it is that the treatment of insanity as if it were only a bodily or even a cerebral disease has been attended with unsatisfactory results. The whole subject of insanity and the current methods of treating it need overhauling, and more rational theories and modes of cure adopted. The world demands it, and is prepared for it.

Insanity is often a loss of magnetic harmony in the brain and nervous system. It is an uncentred mental state and a corresponding unbalanced cerebral condition, portions of the cerebral mass being negative and devitalized, while other parts are positive and crowded with blood and nerve force. Where there is this inharmony in the vital forces of the brain, and their unequal distribution, nothing can be so well adapted to its cure as the psychopathic treatment. This is a specific for all cerebral disturbance. It acts directly upon the brain and nerve tissue, which seem to have an affinity for it, while other remedial agents affect the brain only by a reflex action. No organ in the body can be so readily and quickly affected, and its vital movements so easily controlled by the psychological force, as the brain.

Insanity seems to arise oftentimes from a loss of magnetic life. The nervous force has been exhausted by sexual intemperance and other depleting abuses, or, what frequently happens, the magnetic and psychic force of the patient has been abstracted and unconsciously appropriated by some one or more other individuals. He has been robbed of the subtle vital magnetic element in his organism by a species of human vampirism. It is a singular fact that patients often have an intuitive consciousness of this, and complain of it as the underlying cause of their trouble. This will not be deemed wholly imaginary by any one familiar with the phenomena and laws of the magnetic agent, which sustains so important a relation to the vital force of the brain and the general organic structure. It is a more frequent antecedent and attendant of insanity than many are aware of who have not investigated the subject. Where it is manifestly the case, and a state of magnetic exhaustion, resulting from excess, the reaction from long-continued over-excitement or vampirism, the remedy unerringly indicated is to impart the needed magnetic life. This, especially in the incipient stages of mental disease arising from the above-named causes, will effect a cure in a brief period of time.

Insane persons are almost invariably extremely sensitive to odyllic and magnetic impressions and to all psychological influences. This is owing to the morbid acuteness of the nerves of sensibility. They are affected by the subtle nerve atmosphere of others, and the emanating sphere of persons and things produces psychometric effects upon them far more than in the normal state. This confirms the theory of the identity of insanity with the magnetic state. All this is true of the conscious and unconscious magnetic sleep. The rays of the moon, which Reichenbach proved to be highly charged with a positive odyllic force, affect the insane, as also persons in the somnambulic trance. Hence the word lunacy from *luna*, the moon, as a synonym of insanity. This over-sensitiveness to these invisible and imponderable agents and forces of nature is a characteristic of their abnormal mental state, but one which adapts them to the psychopathic treatment. A distinguished writer on the subject has affirmed, that in many patients the chief symptom is so intense a degree of odyllic and magnetic sensitiveness, that the impressions made on the sensorium by these subtle effluvia and forces are so vivid as to overpower those derived through the medium of the outward senses. This is true of the higher degrees of the magnetic state, and points to the therapeutic effects of magnetism as the sovereign remedy.

Owing to this general characteristic of insanity, it seems many times to be caused, or at least prolonged, by an uncongenial psychological influence which has taken possession of the unhappy subject and holds him in an unwilling bondage. These cases bear a striking resemblance to the obsessions mentioned in the Gospel narratives. The analogy between them has been observed by many in every subsequent century. The patient is often conscious of this disorderly psychological or spiritual influence which controls him. I have met with several cases of the kind, — one, a lady of fifty years of age, who recovered in a week's time, on breaking this mysterious and potent influence, whether imaginary or real, by magnetism. On this subject Dr. Abercrombie remarks: "There seems reason to believe that the hallucinations of the insane are often influenced by a certain sense of the new and singular state in which their mental powers really are, and a certain feeling, though confused and ill-defined, of the loss of that power over their mental processes which they possessed when in health. To a feeling of this kind I am disposed to refer the impression, so common among the insane, of being under the influence of some supernatural power. They sometimes represent it as the working of an evil spirit, and sometimes as witchcraft. Very often they describe it as a mysterious and undue influence which some individual has obtained over them, and this influence they often represent as being carried on by means of electricity, galvanism, or magnetism."

This I doubt not is far from being altogether unreal or the workings of imagination. But whether real or only a disordered fancy, it is only a better and stronger psychological influence, brought to bear upon the case, that can cure it. This in ninety-nine cases in a hundred will succeed after all other means have failed. When the true nature of insanity is better understood, the means of cure, now blindly practised, will be abandoned, and other agencies employed scientifically certain in their beneficial results. It is remarked by Dr. Gregory, that, "Many insane persons appear, when we study the symptoms as they are described by writers on the subject, to be, in fact, only in a peculiar magnetic state. I mean, they have a consciousness distinct from their ordinary consciousness, just as happens in the magnetic sleep." If this be true, and there can be little doubt of its substantial correctness, it is reasonable to suppose that they might be cured, or, in other words, restored to their ordinary consciousness, by a judicious psychopathic treatment. Drug medication would not be a proper method of bringing a person out of the somnambulic state or magnetic sleep. There would be danger by such a course of making the case worse. An intelligent practitioner of Medical Psychology finds no difficulty in doing it. In case of insanity, the patient should be put either into the conscious impressible state or the unconscious sleep. This will usually be easily effected, owing to their more than ordinary susceptible condition.

When accomplished, you have complete control over all their disordered mental manifestations and physical symptoms. We hope the time is not far distant when this agency will be tested, under conditions favorable to its success, and on a scale commensurate with its importance. Public attention is already turned in that direction, and this will ultimate in the supply of so manifest a desideratum. Insanity is often only a state of mental alienation; that is, some influence foreign to the individual has taken possession in a greater or less degree of the patient. In all such cases, owing to the uncongenial and inharmonious nature of the dominating influence, there is more or less spiritual and mental disturbance. In the myriads of cases of this kind, let the disorderly control be supplanted and transferred to the hands of a sympathetic friendship.

INFLUENCE OF KINDNESS.

" How softly on the bruiséd heart
    A word of kindness falls,
And to the dry and parchéd soul
    The moistening tear-drop calls.
Oh! if they knew who walked the earth
    'Mid sorrow, grief and pain,
The power a word of kindness hath,
    'Twere paradise again.

" The weakest and the poorest may
    The simple pittance give,
And bid adieu to withered hearts,
    Return again and live.
Oh! what is life if love be lost?
    If man's unkind to man,
Oh, what the heaven that waits beyond
    This brief and mortal span!

"As stars upon the tranquil sea
 In mimic glory shine,
So words of kindness in the heart
 Reflect the source divine.
Oh! then be kind, whoe'er thou art
 That breathest mortal breath,
And it shall brighten all thy life,
 And sweeten even death."

CHAPTER XXIII.

REMEDIES PARTLY MECHANICAL, PARTLY PSYCHOPATHIC.

Cure of Epistaxis — Pressure of the Femoral Artery — Compression of the Carotids — Cure of Headache — Dizziness — Apoplexy — Epilepsy — Hysteria — Compression of the Vagus Nerve — Its Influence upon the Various Organs — Cure of Nausea — Gastric Inflammation — Sea-Sickness — Laryngitis — Bronchitis — Diphtheria and Croup — Relief of Nervous Excitement — Testimony of Dr. Weller — When to Use Vagal Pressure — How we Learn.

THERE are some remedial processes of a simple character, which produce immediate effects, that act mechanically rather than magnetically. Take, as an illustration, the common-sense cure of *epistaxis*, or bleeding from the nose. In certain cases, as in full-blooded persons, and those subject to dizziness and headache from an excess of blood in the brain, bleeding from the nose may be a salutary relief, and a preventive of apoplexy, and ought not to be checked too hastily. In other cases, when long continued and excessive, it requires instant attention. There is a small artery, called the facial artery, branching off from the great carotid in the neck, which supplies the face and nostrils with blood. It passes outside the lower jaw, about an inch from the angle, where in a slight depression it may be found. Place the finger firmly on the right facial artery, if the bleeding is from the right nostril, and on the left facial artery, if the bleeding is from that side of the nostril, and press it tightly against the bone for five minutes. This shuts off the supply of blood to the affected parts. In a few minutes the ruptured vessels in the nose will contract and the blood in them coagulate, and the cure is effected. This is much better than the application of the various styptics to the parts.

In case of painful inflammations in the lower limbs, pressure upon the femoral artery and the nerve accompanying it will diminish the supply of blood to the affected part, and lessen its sensibility, and thus afford relief. The effects of pressure upon the large carotid artery on each side of the neck were known to physicians in the remotest ages. Caspar Hoffman states "that the Assyrians were in the habit of tying the veins of the neck so as to cause insensibility while performing circumcision upon adults. Aristotle also refers to this mode of producing insensibility. Serapion also mentions the influence of pressure upon the vessels of the neck for the relief of headache. For all derangements originating in an excess of blood in the brain, as headache, dizziness, apoplexy, hysteria, epilepsy, and various nervous disorders, it would seem to be the natural method of relief, to diminish the supply of blood to the brain, by compression of the carotid artery, while the jugular vein which carries off the blood from the head is left unobstructed. This artery may be found just back of the angle of the lower maxillary bone. The pressure need not be carried to the extent of causing insensibility or swooning, but only so far as to lessen rather than suspend entirely the flow of blood to the brain. In this way the restlessness of nervous patients, and their habitual wakefulness, may be relieved, and sleep induced, when the trouble originates in a determination of blood to the head. In all these cases nothing would seem to be more simple or efficient. I have tried it for many years. Dr. Parry, of Bath, England, called the attention of the medical world many years ago to the practical value of compression of the carotids for the relief of violent headache, epilepsy, hysteria, and other disorders.

Much of the effect attributed to compression of the vessels of the neck is now found to be due to the pressure of the vagus or pneumogastric nerve. This, as we have before shown, is one of the most important and widely distributed of the cranial nerves. The pulsations of the carotid artery are the best guide in finding it, as it is in immediate proximity to it, so that when the finger is placed on the artery it involves the nerve in the pressure. The slightest pressure upon the brain, when a portion of the cranium has been removed, causes insensibility. The compression of a nerve diminishes the sensitiveness and lessens the vital action of the part or parts to which it is distributed. The vagus nerve sends branches to the heart, the lungs, the stomach, and other internal organs, and is both a nerve of sense and motion. Compression of this nerve can be made to affect the action of the heart, and arrest palpitation. In all cases where you wish to diminish the action of the heart, you can do it in this way far better and more safely than by the administration of veratrum. You can affect also the action of the diaphragm and lungs, and change the respiration. These are two important points in the treatment of inflammatory diseases.

For the relief of nausea and vomiting, and an oversensitiveness of the gastric membranes, it has been found, by experience, that a better effect is produced by applying the fingers further down on each side where the carotid and nerve pass under the clavicle. This is an efficient remedy for sickness at the stomach and the incipient stages of cholera morbus. My experiments with it for ten years have confirmed me in the opinion of its reliability and certainty. Dr. Augustus Weller, of Geneva, in an article republished in the "Bowdoin Scientific Review," states that he has, by compression of the vagus nerve, relieved himself, on several occasions, of sea-sickness, to which distressing malady he is a martyr. It will be found a more reliable process of relief than the newly recommended chloral hydrate. We have here a remedy of great value, and one applicable to a large range of diseases.

The pneumogastric nerve descends from the medulla oblongata, where it has its origin near the part termed by Fleurens the "*nœud vital*," the vital knot, the most vital part of the cerebral organism, the slightest puncture here being instantly fatal. Near its origin there exists a ganglion, and lower down there is another ganglionic enlargement. Near this, it gives off the superior laryngeal nerve. In sore throat, laryngitis, and even bronchitis, compression of this part of the vagus nerve affords relief. Perhaps we have here a remedy for croup and diphtheria. But I have never tried it in these last-mentioned disorders.

Dr. Weller speaks of the efficiency of vagal pressure in allaying nervous excitement and inducing sleep. He says: " It is particularly efficacious in cases where one pervading idea of an annoying nature occupies the mind, which cannot be dispelled, but is rather intensified, by any attempt to dispel it. Under such conditions the influence of vagal compression is most heroic. Even if sleep is not induced, if once we produce a sense of faintness, by vagal pressure, it seems to act as a sponge passed over writing on a slate, either removing this one ideal state, or bringing the intensified idea on a level with the others. I have repeatedly verified this effect on myself and other persons, by comparing the state of mind before and after vagal compression."

It seems to be a law, that pressure upon a nerve, by sundering the communication between the parts to which it ramifies and the sensorium, lessens the sensibility of those parts, and diminishes their vital action. Knowing when these effects are desirable in an organ, it will be easy to decide when to employ it. Pressure upon the branch of the trifacial nerve, which is distributed to the teeth and jaws, will relieve toothache. It produces temporarily, and in a less degree, the same effect as dividing the nerve. In cases of maniacal excitement, I have a strong conviction that vagal pressure, which must of necessity include compression of the carotid artery, which supplies blood to the brain, would often be productive of the happiest results. It at least deserves a trial. Where there is in such patients an excess of blood in the brain, which is uniformly the case, vagal pressure will undoubtedly produce a quieting influence, much sooner than bromide of potassium and canabis indica, which, when given together, are found to be the best internal remedy. The things recommended in this chapter are to be used only as auxiliaries in the psychopathic treatment. Under the direction of skill and intelligence they will be found efficient remedies. There is much to be learned, which the medical science of the world does not and cannot teach, regarding the nature of disease, and the best method of controlling and regulating the organic forces of the human organism.

HOW WE LEARN.

"Great truths are dearly bought. The common truth,
　　Such as men give and take from day to day,
Comes in the common walk of easy life,
　　Blown by the careless wind across our way.

"Bought in the market, at the current price,
　　Bred of the smile, the jest, perchance the bowl;
It tells no tales of daring or of worth,
　　Nor pierces even the surface of a soul.

"Great truths are greatly won; not found by chance,
　　Nor wafted on the breath of summer dream;
But grasped in the great struggle of the soul,
　　Hard-buffeting with adverse wind and stream.

"Not in the general mart, 'mid corn and wine;
　　Not in the merchandise of gold and gems;
Not in the world's gay hall of midnight mirth;
　　Not 'mid the blaze of regal diadems;

"But in the day of conflict, fear and grief,
　　When the strong hand of God, put forth in might,
Ploughs up the subsoil of the stagnant heart,
　　And brings the imprisoned truth-seed to the light.

"Wrung from the troubled spirit, in hard hours
　　Of weakness, solitude, perchance of pain,
Truth springs, like harvest from the well-ploughed field,
　　And the soul feels it has not wept in vain."

CHAPTER XXIV.

MENTAL MEDICINE, OR THE SANATIVE VALUE OF THE PSYCHIC FORCE.

Supreme Influence of the Mind — The Fundamental Maxim of Christ — Faith and its Influence — Secret of Success in the Psychopathic Treatment — Force of Suggestion — Apollonius of Tyana — Philosophy of the New Testament Miracles — The Medical System of Jesus — Dr. Quimby — How to Remove the Underlying Cause of Disease — The New Psychic Force — Its Sanative Value — Quotation from Dr. Nichols — Appropriation of New Discoveries — Human Progress — The New and Old.

THE interior organism, which we call the mind or spirit, is the controlling element in our complex being, and the living, moving force of the body. The importance of the condition and influence of the inward man has been almost overlooked and ignored in all ages by the practitioners of the healing art. Jesus, the Christ, is the only physician who has ever given, theoretically and practically, due prominence to the spiritual side of human nature in the cure of disease. I know of no other who has done this, in the annals of mankind and the history of medicine. He aimed to restore first the disordered mind to health and harmony, and then through this the outward body. His fundamental maxim was, that a man is saved by faith, soul, spirit and body. The oft-repeated formula, "Be it unto thee according to thy faith," is the key to his whole system of cure, and expresses an important law of our being. The world has never yet comprehended the real relation of the law of faith to the preservation of health and the cure of diseases of mind and body. The science of magnetism has given us exhibitions of its wonderful power in controlling and affecting the bodily organs and their functional movements.

The secret of success in curing disease by vital magnetism and psychopathic remedies is found in the power of what has been denominated suggestion. We have shown, in a previous chapter of this work, that when a person is in the impressible conscious state, a simple suggestion from the operator is capable of controlling all the voluntary movements of the patient, and of influencing at once the physiological action of the various organs of the body. It produces these striking physiological effects, because in that condition the patient has faith, and unhesitatingly believes what is told him, and furnishes an illustration of the operation of the law of faith. Many chronic invalids are more or less in this susceptible condition. If they are not so, they can be easily thrown into the state in which they are extremely sensitive to the action of psychological forces. This explains all that is mysterious in the cures wrought by Jesus, as they are narrated in the gospels. It explains and renders credible also the wonderful cures effected by Apollonius of Tyana, who was born about four years before the commencement of the Christian era, and who is affirmed to have cured the most dangerous diseases with what was deemed a miraculous power. The followers of Apollonius, the Neo-Platonic philosophers, placed his remarkable cures, which seem to have been well authenticated, as a counterbalance to the miracles of Christ. But all these wonders, so far as they are historically true, are explicable by the known laws of magnetism. They were accomplished in harmony with science and nature, but perhaps while ignorant in a good degree of the law by which they were done. The force of suggestion over a patient in the conscious impressible state is the key that unlocks the whole mystery. It explains the miracles of Christ and those of Apollonius. It brings to light the hitherto occult force by which they were effected, and takes them out of the class of miracles by reducing them to the operation of natural law. Here is a principle, an arcane psychic force, worthy of patient study, and one which will repay persevering, honest investigation. Intelligent experimentation with it, will be rewarded by a rich harvest of established principles and results. It opens the secret chambers of knowledge as to the relation of the mind and its states to health and disease.

There is profound philosophy underlying the cures effected by Christ, and a distinct school of medicine may be erected upon it. One of the marked characteristics of the system is the discarding of all drugs and chemical agencies, and the placing sole reliance on psychical forces and remedies. It recognizes the supreme controlling influence of the mind over the body, the inner over the outward man, both in health and disease. The body seems to have been viewed by him, not as the real selfhood, but as only the shadow of the soul, the inner life of man. It corresponds to or echoes the states and movements of the interior nature. Disease is not so much a mere physical derangement, in its primary principle, as it is an abnormal mental condition, an inharmony of the psychical element and force, — a wrong belief, a falsity. This fixed belief, that was viewed as the root of the morbid outward condition, is not a mere intellectual act, and has no reference to a creed, but represents an inward condition, the state of the inner man, what the German writers on the philosophy of mind denominate the interior consciousness. This is the governing element, the controlling principle. The bodily state is the index to it. "As a man thinketh in his heart, so is he." Disease being in its root a *wrong belief*, in the sense explained above, change that belief, and we cure the disease. By faith we are thus made whole. There is a law here the world will some time understand and use in the cure of the diseases that afflict mankind. The late Dr. Quimby, of Portland, one of the most successful healers of this or any age, embraced this view of the nature of disease, and by a long succession of most remarkable cures, effected by psychopathic remedies, at the same time proved the truth of the theory and the efficiency of that mode of treatment. Had he lived in a remote age or country, the wonderful facts which occurred in his practice would have now been deemed either mythical or miraculous. He seemed to reproduce the wonders of the Gospel history. But all this was only an exhibition of the force of suggestion, or the action of the law of faith, over a patient in the impressible condition.

But how can we change that *fixed belief*, that condition of the interior consciousness, that underlies the state of disease? Here is the only practical difficulty in the cure of the disease. When the patient is in the impressible state, a positive *faith* in the physician by a psychological law, invariable in its action, is communicated to the subject, and, as it were, lifts him out of the fixed belief in which he was grounded into a new state. This mental energy and psychic force supplant the weakened power of the patient, to whom they are imparted as the controlling principle. A man's reputation as a successful healer may aid in the generation of this faith in a patient. We are saved by *faith*. This is not only a sound Scripture doctrine, but a settled law of human nature. Whatever assists in the generation and induction of this faith has a sanative value. When the physician is under the influence of a strong, unyielding faith, it is communicated to the patient as readily as an extinguished lamp can be lighted from the flame of another. To change the mental state of an invalid necessarily modifies the condition of the bodily organs and the action of the vital force.

There can be little doubt that the force which is at present attracting the attention of the scientific world, and which has been denominated the psychic force, can be turned to a useful account. This force, whatever its origin, is made to move ponderable bodies, and to play on musical instruments, without any visible agency adequate to produce such effects. It is sometimes sufficient to counteract the utmost power of a strong man. It is manifestly under the direction and control of intelligence. This property of the phenomena is as manifest as the visible effects themselves. This force, as manifested in the presence of the celebrated Mr. Home, has been investigated and experimented with by three men widely known to science,— William Crookes, F. R. S., editor of the " London Chemical News ; " Sergeant Cox, a distinguished member of the English bar ; and the celebrated astronomer, Dr. Huggins. This force they have christened the psychic force. It is new only in the sense that the laws governing it have not hitherto been understood. It has been in the world from the beginning. It is now admitted that there is such an agency. This is as clear as any fact of science, — as chemical affinity or gravitation. And when the laws to which it is subject, and the conditions under which it acts are fully understood, I firmly believe it can be made available for the relief of physical inharmonies, to an extent and with a success of which we scarcely dream at present. My own experiments with it, during the last two years, have served to confirm me in this opinion, though they have not been sufficiently extensive or numerous to enable me to state anything as settled with scientific certainty, but only to create the hope that there is an effectual sanative value in it, which awaits future development. Remarkable facts might be detailed, but are withheld for the present. It will probably operate by means that are invisible, but with results that are tangible. The intelligent psychic force will act upon the human organism through certain intermediate and semi-spiritual principles, as the nerve atmosphere or emanating sphere of certain persons, and the subtle effluvia of all bodies in nature, especially the magnetic and odyllic agencies. The life of all material things, including the human organism, is spirit or psychic force. All force and all causation are immaterial, imponderable, and psychical, as much so as that which moves my hand in writing. There is a psychical or spiritual world discreetly distinct from this, but interfused within it. All the great powers of nature and all the outward phenomena of the material universe are resultants of the action of that world upon this. This is no new truth. According to Diogenes Laertius, Thales taught that " souls are the motive forces of the universe." Empedocles (*Carmina*, v. 11–15), affirms that " spiritual forces move the visible world." Virgil asserts, *mens agitat molem*, mind animates and moves the world. The spiritual realm is the *animus mundi*, the soul of the universe. It is not unreasonable to believe that this grand psychical force, the general sphere of intelligence and life that animates all things, may be made available, under conditions that remain to be studied and discovered, for the cure of disease, and to affect the vital powers of the bodily organism.

On the subject of the psychic force, Dr. Nichols, editor of the "Boston Journal of Chemistry," remarks: "Manifestly there are invisible, imponderable agencies of great power in this world, other than those which modern science recognizes, and it is a source of no little annoyance and mortification that thus far we have failed to bring them within the field of scientific investigation. At present the whole matter is involved in doubt and perplexity, but we have faith to believe that a future age will solve the great mystery and roll away the dark clouds which obscure our vision."

Sometimes a principle is known to science and recognized in the world before it is put to any useful employment. This is true of the so-called psychic force. So the attraction of loadstone for iron was known long before the construction of that useful instrument, the mariner's compass. The action of chlorine on alcohol led to the discovery of a fragrant, volatile liquid, which for more than a score of years was a useless curiosity in the laboratory of the chemist. But in process of time, under the name of chloroform, it was found to produce, when inhaled, insensibility to pain in surgical operations. In the not distant future, more subtle and potent agencies, those that approach nearer the mysterious vital spark, will be employed in the cure of disease. Such is perhaps the psychic force. In the progress of the world and the refinement of mankind, spiritual and psychological agencies will be more employed as sanative agents, and the present gross and barbarous remedies will be discarded. It is the duty of the scientific physician to test the sanative virtue of all new discoveries in the realm of nature, and appropriate them to the relief of human suffering and the cure of mental and bodily disease, so that the practice of the healing art may keep even pace with the advancement of mankind.

The soul of man is constructed on the principle of progress, and human nature, by virtue of the divine and spiritual forces that act from within outward, is slowly but surely being unfolded to a loftier destination. As certainly as the germ of the acorn in a favoring soil and beneath a genial sky will become the sturdy oak, or the early dawn grow into the perfect day, so the infant powers of the mind, and its latent, undeveloped faculties, shall some time expand into full angelhood. The germ of the divine life in man, which lies at the inmost centre of our being, will some time come to dominion, and have everything its own way in our inner and outer nature. Every noble thought, though buried beneath the dust of years gone by, shall have a resurrection to life again and be clothed with immortality. Every good desire is but a prophetic intimation of what shall be. Every bud of lofty aspiration shall blossom into flower and ripen into fruit. Our brightest hopes, our cherished expectations, though they may seem to be blasted, and to have gone down like a star in the darkened west, shall rise again in brightness in the east. They are foregleams of the coming reality, and all our dreams of future good are but a partly veiled prevision of blessings that shall be. The good we seem to have lost is not forever gone, but, like gems long buried in the earth, in some auspicious hour will come to light again with untarnished lustre and undiminished brightness. The blackest cloud that ever settled around us will pass away, and no longer veil the spiritual heavens in darkness, but through it shall break the sun of a higher sky. Our darkest night will end in dawn, and the dawn shall kindle into day. Let us cherish a boundless faith in the good time coming, and let hope for ourselves and the world be as a guiding star upon our life's troubled ocean. If around our bark the waves of sorrow break fierce and high, the voice of infinite Love shall rebuke their rage, and they shall sink like sobbing infants to their rest. While the storm lasts, inspired by hope and courage, put strength to the oar. The long-expected land is just ahead. We shall reach the port to-morrow.

THE OLD AND NEW.

" Oh, sometimes gleams upon our sight,
Through present wrong, the eternal right!
And step by step, since time began,
We see the steady gain of man.

"That all of good the past has had
Remains to make our own time glad,
Our common daily life divine,
And every land a Palestine.

" We lack but open eye and ear
To find the Orient's marvels here;
The still, small voice in autumn's hush,
Yon maple wood, the burning bush.

"For still the new transcends the old,
In signs and tokens manifold;
Slaves rise up men; the Olive waves
With roots deep set in battle-graves.

" Through the harsh noises of the day
A low, sweet prelude finds its way;
Through clouds of doubt and creeds of fear
A light is breaking, calm and clear.

"Henceforth my heart shall sigh no more
For olden time and holier shore;
God's love and blessing, then and there,
Are now, and here, and everywhere."

JOHN G. WHITTIER.

www.ingramcontent.com/pod-product-compliance
Lightning Source LLC
Chambersburg PA
CBHW021914180426
43198CB00035B/536